Yes, You Can Be a Successful Income Investor!

ALSO BY BEN STEIN

HOW TO RUIN YOUR LIFE (hardcover)
(also available as an audio book)

HOW TO RUIN YOUR LOVE LIFE

HOW TO RUIN YOUR FINANCIAL LIFE

HOW TO RUIN YOUR LIFE
(tradepaper that comprises the three titles above)

■■■■

ALSO BY BEN STEIN AND PHIL DEMUTH

CAN AMERICA SURVIVE?:
The Rage of the Left, the Truth, and What to Do about It

YES, YOU CAN STILL RETIRE COMFORTABLY!:
The Baby-Boom Retirement Crisis and How to Beat It
(available September 2005)

■■■■

All of the above are available at your local bookstore, or may be ordered
by visiting the distributors for New Beginnings Press:

Hay House USA: **www.hayhouse.com**
Hay House Australia: **www.hayhouse.com.au**
Hay House UK: **www.hayhouse.co.uk**
Hay House South Africa: **orders@psdprom.co.za**
Hay House India: **www.hayhouseindia.com**

■■■■

Yes, You Can Be a Successful Income Investor!

Reaching for Yield in Today's Market

Ben Stein and Phil DeMuth

NEW BEGINNINGS PRESS
Carlsbad, California

Published by: New Beginnings Press, Carlsbad, California

Distributed in the USA by: Published and distributed in the United States by: Hay House, Inc.: www.hayhouse.com • *Published and distributed in Australia by:* Hay House Australia Pty. Ltd.: www.hayhouse.com.au • *Published and distributed in the United Kingdom by:* Hay House UK, Ltd.: www.hayhouse.co.uk • *Published and distributed in the Republic of South Africa by:* Hay House SA (Pty), Ltd.: orders@psdprom.co.za • *Distributed in Canada by:* Raincoast: www.raincoast.com • *Published in India by:* Hay House Publications (India) Pvt. Ltd.: www.hayhouseindia.com • *Distributed in India by:* Media Star: booksdivision@mediastar.co.in

Editorial supervision: Jill Kramer   *Design:* Summer McStravick

Library of Congress Cataloging-in-Publication Data

Stein, Benjamin, 1944-
    Yes, you can be a successful income investor! : reaching for yield in today's market / Ben Stein and Phil DeMuth.
        p. cm.
    ISBN 1-4019-0319-3 (hardcover) -- ISBN 1-4019-0320-7 (tradepaper) 1. Investments. 2. Finance, Personal. I. DeMuth, Phil, 1950- II. Title.

HG4521.S7554 2005
332.63'2--dc22

2004020174

Hardcover ISBN 13: 978-1-4019-0319-0
Hardcover ISBN 10: 1-4019-0319-3
Tradepaper ISBN 13: 978-1-4019-0320-6
Tradepaper ISBN 10: 1-4019-0320-7

09 08 07 06   7 6 5 4
1st printing, February 2005
4th printing, January 2006

Printed in the United States of America

*For every man and woman who fights now
and has fought to keep us free in this great country,
and for the families who keep them going—alone, often in fear,
sometimes desperate, but always giving far more than they receive.*

Contents

CHAPTER ONE

Welcome to
the Real World

In a nation where the official inflation rate is presently 2.3 percent, the following table shows the yields available on our savings as of this writing.

Table 1.1: Yields on Savings 09/2004	
Source	**Yield**
90-Day T-Bill	1.7%
Average Passbook Savings Account	0.7%
Average 6-Month CD	1.7%
Average Money Market Fund	1.4%
Dow Jones Industrial Average Dividend Yield	2.1%
S&P 500 Dividend Yield	1.8%

In other words, we're earning a *negative* return after inflation and taxes. Still, even in today's low-interest-rate environment, higher yields are available. Look at the income tantalizingly offered by some of the securities on the next page:

Table 1.2: Yields Available 09/2004	
Source	Yield
Preferred Stock:	
Chartwell Dividend & Income Fund	10.1%
Delaware Dividend & Income	8.2%
DNP Select Income	7.0%
John Hancock Patriot Global Dividend	7.1%
John Hancock Preferred Equity Income	8.7%
BlackRock Preferred Opportunity	8.1%
Nuveen Quality Preferred Income Fund	8.2%
Preferred Income Strategies Fund	8.7%
Convertible Securities:	
Gabelli Convertible & Income	8.1%
Calomos Convertible Opportunites	8.8%
Advent Claymore Convertible	8.8%
Municipal Bonds:	
BlackRock Municipal Bond Trust	10.1%
Federated Premier Muni Income	9.9%
Eaton Vance Insured Muni	9.5%
Putnam Muni Opportunities Trust	9.8%
World Income:	
Templeton Emerging Mkts Income	7.7%
Morgan Stanley Global Opportunities	6.2%
Alliance World	6.8%
Salomon World Wide Income	7.9%
Corporate Bond:	
1838 Bond Debenture Fund	6.7%
Lincoln National Income Fund	6.6%
PIMCO Corporate Income Fund	8.2%
Real Estate Investment Trusts:	
Cohen & Steers Premium Income	7.6%
Cohen & Steers Quality Realty	7.9%
Nuveen Real Estate Income	8.6%

Many more examples can (and will) be given. Yet most of us know little, if anything, about these investments. We want to extract the maximum possible income from our savings, and we'd love to earn these kinds of returns. But would our money be safe?

By the time you finish reading this book, you'll know—or at least, you'll know as much as we do. Gone are the days when you could turn over your investments to a bank or a brokerage house and be confident of getting a fair return on your dollar (if those days ever existed). Today, you need to learn everything you can about your money and how to put it to work for you.

Our plan is simple: We're going to talk about a number of different income-yielding securities, and then tell you how to combine them in a portfolio, where we'll endeavor to secure the maximum yield for the least amount of risk.

We're going to name names and be specific, rather than talk in generalities. The investments we call to your attention in this book are all available to ordinary retail investors. Our recommendations are guidelines but by no means exhaustive. They should be good jumping-off points, but there may be others that are superior. Our experience is that simpler is usually better, and that being well diversified and keeping expenses low—two of our goals—will serve you well in the long run.

If we mention a particular investment along the way that has you smacking your lips, please read the entire book before opening your wallet. One of the biggest differences between amateur and professional investors is that professionals have a top-down, "big picture" view of their investment portfolios, while everyone else tends to have a collection of individual securities that struck their fancy at one time or another, but without much regard as to how they all fit together. It makes more sense to decide on your overall strategy first, and then choose the specific investments to park inside it.

The world of income-producing securities is a mysterious jungle. This book is a sightseeing tour bus, pointing out some of the lavish orchids you may wish to acquire for your garden, while steering you away from some of the tigers known to be man-eaters.

Let's start by looking at the circumstances that led us to write it.

CHAPTER TWO

Investing for Yield

In 2000, we could get 6.2 percent interest on a risk-free T-bill. Today, the rate has fallen to 1.7 percent. What happened?

The Federal Reserve Board tried to kick-start the economy after the stock market crash of 2000 to 2002 and the recession of 2000 to 2001 by flooding it with cheap money, and has used a major weapon—the power to set the federal funds rates—to lower them. Thirteen interest-rate cuts took us from 6.5 percent to 1 percent. By the time you read this, interest rates are rising once more—if the Fed's efforts to reflate the economy have proven successful.

In the meantime, for people living off their savings, this collapse has been a double whammy. First, many of them lost a fortune in the stock market crash of 2000 to 2002. Then, as they ran screaming from stocks like teenagers fleeing the Blob in the 1958 horror flick, the yields on their fixed-income investments vaporized. Everyone jumped into the fixed-income lifeboat at once, and it sank.

Retirees clung to the safety of T-bills, CDs, and money market funds to provide them with a secure, steady source of income. They took an 85 percent pay cut—not exactly what any of us want for our old age. This isn't just a statistic, but a figure with serious human consequences: It means cutting out trips to see the family, sending the grandchildren cards instead of presents on their birthdays, selling a diamond ring just to make ends meet, not being able to afford restaurants or movies or socializing with friends, and not getting prescriptions filled. As retirees and others living on fixed incomes confront their incredible shrinking monthly income checks, these low yields translate into loneliness, anxiety, depression, and even shortened life spans.

There's a moral here for the baby-boom generation, which lives on the cusp of retirement today with drastically insufficient savings for tomorrow. First, we have to save, save, save. Then we have to educate ourselves in how to safely squeeze the last drop of yield from our investment dollars.

The Growth Model

For years, people assumed that the stock market would solve their income needs, since it has historically compounded at a nominal rate of about 10 percent per year. All investors had to do was buy a diversified basket of U.S. stocks (such as an S&P 500 Index fund), sell off something *less* than 10 percent every year to meet living expenses, and by simple arithmetic they could tread water virtually indefinitely. The stock market was a cornucopia that would provide all the cash they'd ever need. So the thinking went—even by such "gurus" as Peter Lynch (who managed Fidelity's Magellan Fund with great success).

The promised long-term 10 percent return from stocks was served up like hotcakes on Wall Street, aided and abetted by pop-finance bestsellers like Jeremy Siegel's *Stocks for the Long Run*. Over extended periods of time, stocks have dramatically outperformed all other asset classes: gold, commodities, T-bills, bonds, and real estate; and stock ownership has handily beaten inflation over the long term. Although serious stagflation such as the United States experienced in the 1970s had the effect of cutting the value of the Dow Jones Industrial Average almost in half, during times of more benign inflation, stocks have raced ahead, providing a cushion for investors.

Figure 2.1 shows a plain-vanilla growth portfolio. Note how the stock position is cut with bonds in a 60/40 ratio to smooth out the economic ups and downs. The stocks aren't just from the S&P 500, but also include a little helping of small-capitalization stocks as well. In addition, one third are devoted to foreign markets, diversifying away from U.S. soil (and the U.S. dollar).

Figure 2.1: A Generic Growth Portfolio

This growth-oriented portfolio can be constructed with just three holdings: Vanguard's Total Stock Market mutual fund (ticker: VTSMX), Vanguard's Total International Stock index fund (ticker: VGTSX), and Vanguard's Total Bond Market index fund (ticker: VBMFX). If your employer offers these options on your 401(k) menu, you should kiss your boss at once.

What's Not to Love?

The problem is that for any short-term span, the stocks in this portfolio can't be relied upon to provide investors with the total returns they've come to expect over the long run. There can be periods of 20 years or even longer—possibly much longer—when the total return from investing in the stock market is zero. For someone retiring at age 65, the prospect of a nest egg turning into a goose egg for the next two decades is bone-chilling.

In our book *Yes, You Can Time the Market!*, your authors argued that these eras of low return from equity investing aren't random events, but tend to follow periods when stock values have risen in excess of what might be justified by their historical fundamentals. Unfortunately, we now live in the shadow of such a period. The run-up of financial markets during the 1990s was unprecedented, and while stocks have fallen from their bubble highs, they are still pricey by most fundamental criteria as of this writing. *This means that over the coming 20 years, the total returns from equity investing could fall significantly short of their historical yearly average of 10 percent.*

In fact, there are two likely scenarios, neither of which holds much appeal. One would be for the stock market to fall dramatically. Following a period of consolidation, investment returns would return to their expected "normal" 10 percent per year. A second possibility is for the market to chug along, delivering significantly lower total returns than usual.

Unfortunately, we aren't the only ones who see it this way. Writing in the *Financial Analysts Journal*, Robert Arnott and Peter Bernstein, two of the brighter crayons in the box, have deconstructed the annualized 10 percent total return that stocks have historically offered. First, they throw out the profit due to inflation, which cuts the real return down to less than 7 percent. This remaining amount has historically consisted primarily of dividends—about five percentage points in all. Seventy percent of the stock market's real return has come from the dividends that stocks have paid.

Why is this a problem? Because today, the dividend yield is abysmally low: Instead of 5 percent, it's a measly 1.8 percent. This implies a total inflation-adjusted stock market return of closer to 3 or 4 percent going forward.

In other words, we're well advised not to rely entirely on the growth model to buy groceries and pay the rent.

The Alternative: Income Investing

If capital appreciation from the stock market isn't going to save us, what might?

Income investing.

This approach might be the answer to where to put our money

when the stock market is just too expensive. Instead of shoveling our dollars into its gaping maw, we could invest them in income-producing securities. When everyone else is feverishly buying into growth that might happen extremely slowly (if at all), we could put our money into income. Or, to put it another way, if we want consistent income, we need investments that yield income fairly consistently. Capital gains are by nature uncertain and speculative, while income investments aren't. For this reason, we're going to advocate that investors seeking a steady paycheck put a substantial portion of their assets into an income-oriented portfolio.

To start this process, we're going to roll up our sleeves and help you learn a bit about the bond market—something you may have hoped to avoid. Then we're going to hunt for stocks that are bucking the trend by paying above-average dividends. We'll also take a hard look at some investment products that promise to deliver an enhanced stream of income to your bank accounts. If risk-free investing gets you less than 2 percent (and a *negative* return after inflation and taxes), you have to decide what risks are worth taking and which ones should be avoided. During the stock market bubble, everyone focused on the rewards of investing, paying scant attention to the risks. Then the NASDAQ blew up in their faces like an exploding cigar. The prudent investor is forever weighing the certainty of risk against the possibility of reward.

In the chapters ahead, we'll describe the basic building blocks of fixed-income investing. We'll tell you the ones we like—and steer you away from some we don't. Then we'll put it all together in some model portfolios that match your income requirements with your tolerance for risk.

We'll even throw in a free Website **(www.stein-demuth.com)**, which we hope will be useful to you. If sharp-eyed readers point out any dumb mistakes we've made, we'll post them, and if we cite a Website in this book, there will be a link to it from our Website so that you don't have to worry about remembering it. Just bookmark **www.stein-demuth.com** and our magic carpet will take you there.

Here's a basic principle to keep in mind as we get started: The most basic way we compare income securities with one another is by comparing their *yields*. This is the amount of income they pay out, divided by their price. If a security pays $5 in interest a year, and it costs $100, its yield is 5 percent.

Unfortunately, yields are not calculated in the same way all over town. When we punch the ticker of a given security into three different Websites today to learn its yield, we get three different answers: 7.2 percent, 7.0 percent, and 6.9 percent. Who's right?

The answer is: They all are—but each one calculates the yield in a slightly different way. One takes the total amount of income a security has generated over the past year and divides this by today's price. Another takes the last quarterly income payment, multiplies it by four, and divides it by today's price. The next takes one of these income calculations and divides it by the price of the security at the end of the last month. Still others may not refer to a true dividend yield, but a "distribution" dividend, which includes all the income from the investment, such as dividends, capital gains, and even a return of principal. In addition, there's also the 30-day SEC yield, which the Securities and Exchange Commission requires to be presented in any advertising literature where a yield is cited. Be aware that money market funds calculate their yields on the last seven days, while bonds have their yield-to-call, yield-to-maturity, and yield-to-worst (whichever of the previous two is lower).

Enough, already!

In truth, we don't really need to know how each of these is calculated, or even which formula a particular source is using. Instead, we simply need to make sure that we're comparing like to like when sizing up potential investments that are competing for our investment dollar. Remember:

1. Use the same source for all yield information. Don't assume that the yield you see quoted on Morningstar is the same as what you see on Yahoo! Finance or read in *Barron's*. By getting all your quotations for the same type of security from the same information service, you can make head-to-head comparisons.

2. The yield refers to the past month or quarter or year, and doesn't tell you what the yield will be *next* month or quarter or year. We can't know the future. Investing is about rational probabilities, not certainties.

3. Some of the information in this book is time sensitive. The yields on many of the investments we cite here will surely be different by the time you read this. Even so, the same general principles will apply.

We'll begin with the classic income investment: bonds. Before making specific recommendations, we want to prepare the groundwork by talking a little bit about what bonds are and how they work. That way, when we do make suggestions, you'll understand our reasoning. We also want to give you the knowledge you need about income-bearing securities so that you can make your own intelligent selections. Although we throw in plenty of "fish" along the way, our real goal is to teach you *how* to fish—and how to feed yourself for life.

CHAPTER THREE

Bond Basics

Many people shy away from learning about bonds because these securities seem so complicated. In our experience, even investors with multimillion-dollar stock portfolios can be as ignorant as swans when it comes to the bond market. This is too bad, because all the esoteric bond lingo masks a few simple ideas that anyone can understand. At the risk of offending bond sophisticates, we think it's best to start with the basics.

Everything you really need to know about bonds can be derived from contemplating the following example:

Our (hypothetical) boss, Mr. Sterling, owner of 50 apartment buildings and the local oil refinery, has come to our home for dinner. After a sufficiently pleasant evening, he takes his hat to go but then pauses at the door. It seems he gave the last $20 bill in his wallet to a homeless person he met on the street, and this leaves him without cab fare. Could he borrow $20 until tomorrow morning, when he'll go to the ATM and pay us back?

We lend him the money without further ado.

No sooner does he leave, but our unemployed brother-in-law rings the doorbell. Stinking of gin, he's in debt again. However, he has a surefire tip for the fifth race at Saratoga tomorrow. As much to get rid of him as anything else, we hand over a double sawbuck. He in turn promises to pay us back double our money. "This time I really mean it," he says.

Congratulations. You now understand the bond market. However, just as in *The Wizard of Oz*, where Dorothy didn't immediately realize that everything she needed was already in her own backyard, you may not know that you already understand the bond market. Let's connect the dots from the example we just gave you.

A bond is an I.O.U., and it contains four essential ingredients:

1. The identity of the borrower
2. A promise to repay the principal
3. The date when it will be repaid
4. The rate of interest it will pay

Mr. Sterling promised to repay our loan the very next day. The interest is zero percent, perhaps because he didn't want to insult us by offering to pay interest on such a trivial sum. Our brother-in-law is going to return our principal and interest at . . . well, come to think of it, he didn't say, did he? At some nebulous time far in the future, a time that may never come, he's going to pay us double.

In the pages of *The Wall Street Journal*, a bond is described in shorthand, like this:

AT&T 6¾ 2008

But the same four bases are touched: who's issuing it (AT&T, a large telephone company), the annual rate of interest on the par or original-issue amount that it promises to pay (called the bond's *coupon* rate, here 6¾ percent, paid in semiannual installments, totaling $67.50 annually), and the date when the principal (usually a $1,000 per bond par amount) will be repaid: 2008.

The essential risk factors in bond investing are as follows:

- *Interest-rate risk:* the risk that other bonds issued later will pay more interest

- *Inflation:* the risk that when the bond is paid back, the dollars it commands will be worth less than when the bond was issued

- *Default:* the risk that either the interest or principal on the bond won't be paid because the issuer falls on hard times

Buyers have devised ways to deal with all of these risks. Typically, the riskier the investment, the higher the yield it will have to pay to attract buyers. Long bonds, for example, usually pay more interest than short-term ones.

The yield curve expresses this feature of the bond market, as in Figure 3.1, which shows the bond yields available as of September 2004 from Treasury securities of differing maturity dates. This curve will surely look different by the time you're reading this, but it still illustrates how shorter maturities typically earn lower yields, while longer maturities earn higher ones.

Figure 3.1: The Yield Curve 09/2004

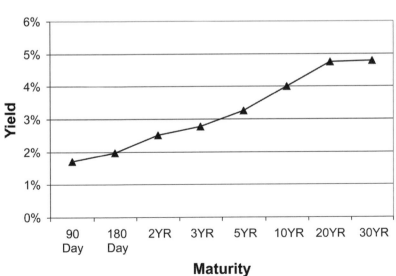

Inflation risk is also addressed by the pairing of longer-term bonds with higher yields, since longer-term bonds have a longer time during which they may be eroded by inflation, and hence they must offer higher yields as compensation.

Bond lenders also demand higher yields from worse credit risks. In the past, as the U.S. economy grew, people wanted to know just how safe money would be that they lent to far-flung enterprises. For this reason, John Moody got into the business of rating bonds in 1909, and Standard & Poor's, Fitch, and Duff & Phelps all got into the act later. Each firm has slightly different ways of issuing report cards, but they basically range from an "AAA" rating for the highest "Mr. Sterling" quality down to "C" for outright junk like our brother-in-law's promises (see Table 3.1). Within each grade, the more letters the better.

Table 3.1: Bond Ratings		
	Standard & Poor's	**Moody's**
Investment Grade	AAA	Aaa
	AA	Aa
	A	A
	BBB	Baa
Speculative Grade	BB	Ba
	B	B
	CCC	Caa
	CC	Ca
	C	C

Older readers who recall when schools actually graded students on their academic performance should grasp the concept instantly. Not every bond is rated, however, as the issuer must pay for this service. If the outcome is a foregone conclusion, for reasons good or bad, then a formal rating may never be obtained.

Figure 3.2 shows the credit-quality curve as of September 2004. The point: Yields rise as credit quality declines, as compensation for the greater risk of default. U.S. Treasury bonds, having virtually no risk of default, pay the lowest yield of all.

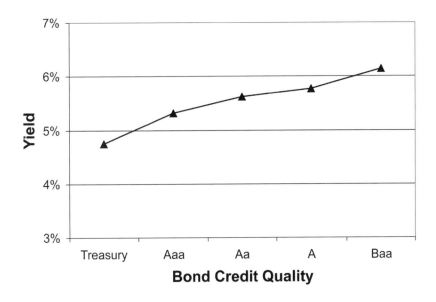

Figure 3.2: The Credit Curve 09/2004

As investors, we all expect to be paid more for lending money to riskier enterprises, and we also expect higher interest the longer our funds are tied up. Long-term, poor credit-quality bonds offer immense nominal coupons; short-term insured CDs pay almost nothing; and there are many intermediate positions.

Who Issues Bonds?

Any institution that wants to borrow your money does so. Over the years, we've noticed that virtually every institution believes it has a good use for more money, including:

- Governmental entities, such as:
  — The federal government
  — Various agencies associated with or run by the federal government
  — Municipal governments: city, county, and state

- Corporations

Let's take a look at how investing with each of these entities works.

Governmental Entities

1. The Federal Government: Since the government has unlimited power to tax its citizens, and the Federal Reserve controls the printing presses, there's every reason to believe that our loans to this institution will be repaid, at least nominally. To put it another way, if for some reason the U.S. government is unable to pay its debts, it's unlikely that any of your assets—your home, your stock certificates, the gold bullion hoarded in your attic—would be particularly secure. Short of living in a cabin in the Yukon with a shotgun and a supply of canned food, there's no way to prepare for the sort of calamity that would result in Uncle Sam defaulting.

The government funds the fabled national debt by issuing bonds—getting spending money today while shifting the costs to future generations who will have to repay it. In some cases, this may be a worthwhile trade-off. For example, were it not for spending money to maintain a strong national defense, there might be no country for a future generation to inherit. Balanced against this, though, is all our money doled out to special interest voting blocs by politicians blatantly seeking reelection. Here's a simple truism that you can stitch into a sampler: The government always thinks it can spend your money on your behalf far more intelligently than you can. But it does have superb credit.

2. Agencies Associated with the Government: While you may tend to think of the federal government as monolithic, it's really more like a group of fiefdoms or anthills, each with its own mission and set of bureaucrats bent on perpetuating itself and expanding its empire. Some of these even have the power to issue bonds to raise money (gulp!). For example, in the first part of the last century, when agriculture was at the heart of the American enterprise, the Federal Farm Credit Consolidated System began underwriting low-interest loans to farmers, and they're still at it today.

Agencies such as these are started to address a specific problem at one point in time (such as the Tennessee Valley Authority, begun during the Great Depression, or the Resolution Trust Corporation, created in 1989 to bail out the Milken-era failed Savings and Loan institutions), but once they're up and running, they have a way of perpetuating themselves forever.

The government believes that its citizens should own their own homes, and so has set up several agencies to underwrite mortgage loans: the Government National Mortgage Association (GNMA, or Ginnie Mae), the Federal National Mortgage Association (Fannie Mae), and the Federal Home Loan Mortgage Corporation (Freddie Mac), among others. The creative accounting and potentially explosive use of derivatives at Fannie Mae and Freddie Mac are legendary, such that they now operate almost as hedge funds.

(One of your authors wishes to express his gratitude to the Student Loan Marketing Association [Sallie Mae] for lavishing tens of thousands of dollars in subsidized loans on his 29-year-old daughter to make student films at UCLA. If the government places such value on higher education, who are we to question this vital use of taxpayer money?)

These government agencies, some of them now privatized, issue bonds that live in the glittering aura of the United States government. That is to say, except for those issued by Ginnie Mae, that they don't formally carry the full faith and credit of the government behind them since they're now run by private business. Nonetheless, it's widely believed that the government (that is, we, the taxpayers) would step in and bail them out should disaster befall. Let us all pray that we never have to find out if this is the case. This situation makes agency debt somewhat less secure than treasury-department debt, but it's still considered to be of "AAA" quality.

Bond mutual funds often have the words *Federal* or *Government* in their titles, and buyers may blithely assume that these are stocked full of U.S. Treasury bonds, when in fact they're larded with paper from Freddie Mac and Fannie Mae—agencies that may or may not be bailed out if a problem develops—and often contain debt that has zero to do with any government at all. If you want U.S. Treasury notes, you have to look for the word *Treasury* in the title. Even so, the funds may include GNMA bonds as well, but at least these are backed by the full faith and credit of the United States (since Ginnie Mae is still owned by the government).

3. Municipal Governments: State and local governments also have an appetite for spending money, so they issue bonds to pay for their various schemes. At present, there are some 1.7 million individual municipal bonds out there, issued by 50,000 municipal entities. Since these governments or their instrumentalities sometimes have the power to levy taxes, their bonds can be highly regarded in terms of credit quality. Some are backed up with more taxing power than others are, and so some municipal bonds are far riskier than others—that is, some are gilt and some are garbage. During the Great Depression, 30 percent of municipal bonds defaulted, and 78 percent of these were initially rated "AA" or higher.

Municipal bonds include:

— **General Obligation Bonds** are backed by the full faith, credit, and taxing power of the issuer. In the worst case, bondholders can compel the state or municipality to hold a tax levy or make a legislative appropriation to meet its debt payments.

— **Revenue Bonds** are less secure, as they're backed only by the promise of revenue flowing from the project they were issued to pay for. If the toll road or the stadium or the sewer makes money, all is well; if not, all bets are off.

— **Special Purpose Bonds,** as for nursing homes or junior colleges, are even less secure than revenue bonds, yet they rarely default.

Think about the caliber of people who get elected to local office—how they may be unemployable elsewhere and yet have command of millions and millions of dollars of taxpayers' money to experiment with—and you may be correct to hesitate before placing all your money in municipal bonds.

Since the 1970s, municipal bonds have been able to buy insurance to placate nervous investors. This sounds good, but it shouldn't provide us with an unlimited measure of relief. As Martin D. Weiss points out in *The Ultimate Safe Money Guide*, the most corrupt town in the country, whose mayor wants to funnel a new bridge project to his nephew, can instantly purchase "AAA" bond ratings through the expedient of buying municipal-bond insurance. Most investors will never be able to learn the pre-insurance rating. There are only a few municipal bond insurers, and every project they underwrite is automatically alchemized to the insurer's own high rating. If massive defaults occur, the lawyers will sit down at the table to feast on the carcass first. How much will be left over for the poor bondholders after the feeding frenzy is anyone's guess.

Because one branch of the government thoughtfully doesn't tax another, the great appeal of municipal bonds is their freedom from federal taxes. If the bonds are from your home state, you may duck the state and local taxes as well . . . so far.

This tax exemption is not inscribed in the Constitution. Congress could elect to change it with the stroke of a pen—although this would make a number of rich political contributors unhappy. We'll return to the subject of taxes later, but in the meantime, there's one more category of bond issuer that interests us.

Corporate Bonds

Corporations are often eager for money. All that trading every day that has Microsoft up or down three points doesn't put any coin directly into the company's coffers (although its shareholders benefit when the stock goes up). Microsoft could issue more stock if they wished, but this would make existing shareholders upset, as it would dilute the value of their outstanding shares. If Microsoft ever wanted to raise more cash, they could float a bond issue and troll for capital from bond-market investors. There are many good reasons for corporations to issue debt by doing this, generally all under the heading that the company thinks that it can use the capital to make more money than the interest it will eventually have to pay on the bond.

Corporate debt can be *secured* or *unsecured*. If secured, specific assets of the corporation are pledged against it (such as the land the factory is built on, or machinery and equipment), while unsecured corporate debt is backed solely by the company's promise to repay. One big advantage corporate bondholders have over stockholders is that they're first in line when it comes to picking over the company's assets in the event of liquidation.

Because corporate debt is less secure than government or municipal debt, Moody's, Standard & Poor's, and other rating agencies stand ready to advise investors on the creditworthiness of a company's bond issues. A high grade means that the corporation will have to pony up less interest to attract investors, but corporate bonds uniformly pay more interest than Treasury notes. That's just a rule of life.

What Is the Bond Market?

The total U.S. bond market, valued at some $15 trillion (give or take a dollar), is larger than the American stock market, but doesn't share the stock market's glamour. There's no cable channel that touts bonds all day long, and this is because the trading of these securities operates differently.

The stock market is organized via large clearinghouses like the New York Stock Exchange. People wishing to buy or sell go there, and every stock listed on it has a specific dealer who operates a market in that security. Stocks can be briskly bought and sold, with prices set by the hue and cry of the open market, or by electronically matching buyers and sellers. Commissions are explicitly stated: They can be less than $10 and rarely are more than 2 percent of the sale price, even at full-service brokerages.

The bond market, by comparison, is decentralized. Corporations might have one class of stock, but can and do issue dozens of types of bonds, each with different characteristics. Because trading of some bonds is infrequent (some issues might not move for months at a time), prices are often arrived at by triangulation—like pricing Renoirs at Sotheby's. The bond trader looks at what similar issues have sold for recently and channels a number, which is the price that we, the buyers, will pay. Conveniently, his or her commission is wrapped into that price and not broken out for separate inspection.

Should you be concerned that the party representing the seller may have inadequately compensated him- or herself for the privilege of selling you the bond? Worry not. The commission might be anywhere from 2 percent to 9 percent. When Bill Gross calls from PIMCO and wants to buy $20 million worth of some security (and the seller hopes he'll call again tomorrow), he gets one price. When you tap on the windowpane with $1,000 to spend, you won't get the same deal.

Here's a thought: Why not order the bond from your broker at Merrill Lynch, Smith Barney, or the like? Surely, with all their clout, they'll make a monkey out of that bond trader and get you a great deal at a rock-bottom price. Unfortunately, this outcome isn't inevitable. A major wire house will seek to fill your order from their own inventory. They may draw your attention to a bond issue they personally underwrote, where their profit can be exceptional. Failing that, they may try to sell you a bond from the portfolio of an existing customer, who might take a significant markdown, upon which you, in turn, will pay a significant mark*up*. If you insist on a specific bond that they don't have on hand, they'll buy it from a competitor and then resell it to you. If they have a lot of nerve, they'll even tell you that they aren't charging a commission (since their markup is already built into the price), perhaps acting like they've done you a great favor. Someday, an Eliot Spitzer type will clean the Augean stables of the bond traders, but for now, this is the reality. These kinds of spreads are why F. Scott Fitzgerald had Nick Carraway enter the business in *The Great Gatsby*, on the supposition that ". . . it could support one more single man." Fidelity Investments, however, has recently announced that it will offer their brokerage customers explicit commissions and let them know a bond's last sale price. This is a welcome move in the right direction.

With all these convolutions, should you *really* venture into the bond market? In the next chapter, we'll weigh the risks and the rewards.

CHAPTER FOUR

Risks and Rewards
of Bond Investing

Y ou may have heard that stocks are risky but bonds are safe. This is only half true: Yes, stocks *are* risky, but bonds are plenty risky, too. If you lose half your money investing in long-term government bonds, it will be of little consolation to have someone tell you that they weren't supposed to be *that* risky.

Risks of Bond Investing

Here again, just to be sure you're warned, is the rogues' gallery of shocks that bonds are heir to, some of which we mentioned briefly in the last chapter.

Interest-Rate Risk

Interest-rate risk is the bond's public enemy number one. The value of a bond, with its fixed coupon, will fluctuate as interest rates change in the outside world. This is because *bond prices and interest rates move in opposite directions.* This "looking-glass land" feature of bonds is what makes them so confusing. When interest rates go up, bond prices fall; when interest rates fall, bond prices go up. Think of them on a teeter-totter, and you'll have it exactly. The constant supply and demand for financial instruments in the open market necessitates that bond prices stay in equilibrium with current interest rates: The interest rate calls the tune, and bonds dance to it.

Suppose, for example, that you bought a 30-year, $1,000 bond with a 5 percent coupon rate, paying $50 a year. Then, a month later, imagine (however unlikely) that 30-year bonds pay 10 percent coupon, or $100 a year. Your old bond will fall in price until it yields roughly the same as the new one, or 10 percent. In other words, its price will fall to about $500. You'll still be repaid $1,000 in full if you hang on until it reaches maturity in 30 years, but for the present, all anyone will pay for it is about $500. Why should they settle for a lower rate than they could get from a brand-new bond?

If your bond had a short maturity, you wouldn't suffer as much, and the pain would end sooner. Short-maturity bonds don't fluctuate nearly as much as long-maturity bonds when interest rates change because they'll be repaid sooner, and the proceeds can be reinvested at the current, higher rate.

The interest-rate risk cuts both ways, though. Had you bought this 5 percent long bond and interest rates immediately fell to 2.5 percent, you'd be pretty smug with your fixed 5 percent bond, and you might be able to sell it for twice what you paid for it. When interest rates decline, bond prices rise.

Interest-rate risk cuts across most of the securities mentioned in this book to some degree. When interest rates rise, existing income-bearing securities—including dividend-paying stocks and real estate investment trusts—tend to fall in value until a new equilibrium is reached.

One defense against interest-rate risk is to diversify it over time, such as by purchasing a *bond ladder*. You can do this by buying individual bonds that mature in successive years, and then replacing the bonds on the lowest rung as they mature with new ones at the highest rung.

For example, you might buy five Treasury notes: one each maturing in 2006, 2007, 2008, 2009, and 2010. When 2006 arrives and that note matures, take your $1,000 return of principal and buy a new Treasury note maturing in 2011. In 2007, roll over the principal from the note maturing that year and buy a five-year Treasury note maturing in 2012. In the interim, you pocket the coupons the notes pay. Financial columnist Scott Burns has pointed out that a simple ladder of five-year Treasury notes regularly trounces most intermediate-term bond funds.

Please understand that the dates we used in the preceding paragraph were arbitrary. You might buy bonds laddered over a ten-year period if you choose, and instead of rolling them over every year, you might purchase notes maturing every two years, just to cut down on the paperwork. The big idea is that by spreading your bets over the entire period, you never wager more than a fraction of your money on the interest rates prevailing in any given year. If rates are low now, perhaps next year will be better. By the way, you aren't limited to bonds: You can also ladder certificates of deposit and fixed annuities, if you wish.

Purchasing-Power Risk

Because of inflation, the dollars you get back when your bond matures usually won't buy as much as they did when you invested them originally. When inflation hit the U.S. during the 1970s, people living on fixed incomes found that the pension check they retired on in 1965 could only buy half as much by 1977. That's purchasing-power risk in spades.

While what happened in the 1970s is a dramatic example, the insidious effects of even low inflation are also terrible for fixed-income investors. Inflation gnaws like a rat at our stored treasure. Consider an inflation rate of 3 percent, often thought of as "benign" (and below the long-term postwar average): If you're living on a fixed income, over the course of 23 years your purchasing power will be sawed in half. In other words, a $1,000 check would only buy $496 worth of groceries. Yet, two decades later, you still may want to eat three meals a day, not one and a half.

Unlike bondholders, bond *issuers* love inflation because it means that they can get expensive money today and repay it with cheap dollars tomorrow. Consider this: The biggest bond issuer in the world is the U.S. government. Does this mean that it has a stake in promoting inflation? Absolutely. Like everyone else, it loves to borrow dear and pay back cheap. Furthermore, politicians have figured out that a little inflation makes many voters feel good. As wages rise, people have the illusion that they're doing better—even though they end up giving it all back and more on the expense side. Best of all, the rising income jacks many people into higher tax brackets, so politicians can raise taxes invisibly, without having to legislate tax increases and suffer the consequences at the polls.

Fortunately, other powerful interests stand shoulder to shoulder with bondholders against inflation. Retirees and wealthy people living on fixed incomes hate inflation. These folks are well connected and politically powerful, although by no means omnipotent. The stock market (the corporations whose stocks are traded as well as the people who own stock) also detests inflation, as it makes the stream of future dividends that stock ownership delivers worth less and less, driving down the price of shares today. Moreover, the noise of inflation drowns out the signal of vital information about supply and demand contained in prices, making it difficult for businesses to plan effectively or maintain reserves to cover depreciation.

Individuals face the same difficulty planning for the future when the threat of inflation hovers. To remedy this situation, the government has begun issuing Treasury Inflation Protected (or Inflation-Indexed) Securities or TIPS, as they're called. We'll have much more to say about these later, as they're the main bond market antidotes to purchasing-power risk.

Occasionally, we hear about the threat of deflation to our economy. While falling interest rates increase the value of fixed bond coupons, in an outright deflationary environment, not all types of bonds fare equally well. Corporate notes are more vulnerable, since companies may have difficulty servicing their higher fixed-debt payments with profits earned later in deflated dollars. But the U.S. Treasury, with the printing press on its premises, will continue to pay its bondholders unencumbered by such concerns. Deflation makes Treasuries the bond investment of choice, and long-maturity Treasury bonds fare best of all.

Credit Risk

This is the risk that the bond issuer won't make its interest and principal payments as promised. In the worst case, the issuer might default and leave the bondholder with nothing. Or, it may undergo reorganization, and the bondholder will be forced to accept less than he or she bargained for. Either scenario would be bad news if you held the bond and wished to sell it.

However, lesser credit risks also apply. If you own an "AAA" corporate bond and it's downgraded to "AA," this will also be reflected in the price. On the other hand, if you bought a "BAA" rated corporate bond and it's upgraded to an "A" rating by Moody's, you stand to benefit.

Government bonds are considered to be risk free, but in reality, nothing is completely risk free. Prudent, safety-conscious Germans who put money into their government's T-bills and bonds in 1921 found that they'd become worthless by 1923 due to hyperinflation. Closer to home, perhaps you've seen the pink-paper currency issued by the Confederate States of America during the Civil War. Pretty in pink though these bills may be, they don't buy what they used to at the Piggly Wiggly. Going back still further, the Continental dollars a fledgling Congress issued in 1776 to finance the Revolutionary War became worthless almost immediately. However, modern British and U.S. Treasury bonds have never defaulted and are as close to being free of this hazard as anything gets.

The chief way to guard against credit risk is by holding either Treasury notes or a diversified portfolio of individual bonds (such as in a bond mutual fund) with a high credit rating. That way, even if one security defaults, the others should still pay off. We'll talk more about this later in the book.

Marketability Risk and Liquidity Risk

These terms mean that you might not be able to easily sell the bond that you bought. There are a variety of factors at work in these cases: The size of the offering might have been small, there may have been few takers, not many people may trade it, and customers may be in short supply. All these factors (which your broker can sometimes fail to mention at the time of purchase) could conspire to make it difficult to sell a bond unless you're willing to accept a lower price. Generally, older and longer-term bonds of low credit quality are the most difficult to unload, while U.S. Treasury notes are easily bought and sold. For these and other reasons, we'll talk about bond mutual funds soon.

Call Risk

Some bonds are subject to call risk, which might also be termed *prepayment risk*. The certificate of a *callable* bond says that the issuer can prepay it at some specified future date, should he or she choose to do so. If interest rates have fallen since it was issued, there's every chance that the bond will be called (just as we all might be inclined to refinance our mortgages if mortgage rates fell). This leaves bondholders, stuck with their money back, having to find some new use for it in a new, lower-interest-rate environment. Of course, this risk was factored into the price of the bond in the first place. If we have a callable bond and interest rates rise, however, the issuer won't find it profitable to call it. Not all bonds are callable, so make sure you read the fine print. The answer to this danger is either to not buy callable bonds, or to be aware of how the call options could affect your portfolio. This may not be as easy as it sounds. Recently, bondholders in Florida learned that some of their municipal bonds had "extraordinary call provisions," allowing the bonds to be called in the event of a calamity such as a hurricane. If you propose to buy individual bonds, get out the magnifying glass and read the fine print—which may go on for hundreds of pages.

Event Risk

This is the possibility that some external event will affect the value of your bond. For example, if you own a municipal revenue bond that's backed by income from the stadium where your local team plays, and that beloved team moves elsewhere and leaves behind an empty stadium, you may well wonder where your next coupon will come from. Or, what happens if United Airlines folds up its operations at that vital new airline terminal that you lent the city money to build? The possible calamity need not even occur, since just the threat of an untoward event can affect a bond's price. Once again, diversification comes to the rescue: By holding a broad spectrum of bonds, such as in a bond mutual fund, you lessen the risk that any one unfortunate event will greatly reduce your portfolio's value.

Sector Risk

The value of your bond may be affected by the fate of the industry sector to which it belongs. For example, during the 19th century, canal bonds—which seemed sound as a dollar at the time— fell in value when railroads put the canals out of business. Even if you'd owned a whole portfolio of bonds from different canals, your lot wouldn't have improved when the entire sector went down the drain. Building the railroads required a mammoth amount of capital, and its pursuit helped give rise to the modern bond market. Later, the automobile and airplane had a similar influence on the value of railroad bonds. The same medicine applies: Holding a diversified portfolio of bonds across sectors lessens the risk that the demise of any one industry will wipe you out. Most bond mutual funds have managers who are constantly buying and selling to meet the fund's objectives, considerably lessening the risk that the portfolio of railroad bonds you bought to pay for retirement will lead to a dark tunnel.

Regulatory/Legislative Risk

If the government decides to change the way bond interest is taxed, you can bet that this will affect the value of bonds. If the after-tax value of the interest payments goes up or down, bond prices will change accordingly. Even if the government changes the way competing investments are taxed, the vibrations will resound in the bond market. Since stocks and bonds vie against each other for investors' money, the recent lowering of the tax on stock dividends in the Jobs and Growth Tax Relief Reconciliation Act of 2003 had the effect of making bond ownership less desirable, since no parallel change was made lowering taxes on bond income.

The main legislative risk before the bond market is that Congress could decide to tax municipal bonds. A lot of rich political donors would be affected, which makes it unlikely, but if times get tough, even this could change. For example, a senator could stand up and make a speech about how all those rich people who own municipal bonds need to start giving something back to America. With Congressional action threatening, it would be too late to get out unscathed. The theory of diversification preaches that you shouldn't put all your money into any one class of bonds, including municipal bonds (let alone single-state municipal bonds). We don't care what tax bracket you're in: Buy some taxable bonds and pay the damned taxes.

Reinvestment Risk

A falling-interest-rate environment subjects you to the risk that you won't be able to reinvest the income from your bond at the same high yield at which you initially secured it. This subjects you to a progressively lower yield over time, as you're forced to reinvest your principal at new, lower rates. This has been the story of the last 20 years, and the compensation is that long-term bonds have appreciated in price during this time, equaling the total return from the stock market. There is no ultimate defense against reinvestment risk unless you want to buy 100-year bonds (Disney offers some), which we don't recommend.

Opportunity Cost

As if all these risks weren't enough, there's also opportunity cost, which is the possibility that you could have done better had you invested your money elsewhere. When talking of bonds, this usually refers to the alternative of the stock market, because over long periods of time, stocks have outperformed bonds. Overall, the 20th century was terrific for stocks and awful for bonds, but we don't know how the 21st century will go. In other countries and at other times, returns from ownership (stock investing) versus "loanership" (bond investing) have been much closer. For all the hoopla about stocks, over the past seven years the Lehman Brothers Aggregate Bond Index has outperformed the S&P 500 Stock Index 7.1 percent to 4.5 percent in annual gain.

Investing for income is *not* getting something for nothing. By receiving a reliable dividend or coupon, you're trading some of the prospect of future growth (such as you might achieve in the stock market) for the certainty of current income. Bonds are for those of us who want a hamburger today, not the promise of a hamburger Thursday. If you're a bondholder and the Dow goes to 36,000, you won't join the party (just as if it falls to 3,600, you won't attend the funeral). You may feel happy or sad about the course of events, depending on how the future unfolds, but at the time when you decided to forego future growth for current income, the decision was a perfectly rational one.

Table 4.1 summarizes the risks that bond investors face and how you can cope with them.

Table 4.1: Bond Risks and What to Do about Them

Risk	Antidote
Interest-Rate Risk	Short Maturities, Ladders, Diversification
Deflation	Treasuries, Diversification
Inflation	Treasury Inflation-Indexed Bonds, Short Maturities, Diversification
Credit Risk	Treasuries, Diversification
Marketability Risk	Open-Ended Bond Funds, Treasuries, Diversification
Call Risk	Read Prospectus, Diversification
Event Risk	Diversification
Sector Risk	Diversification
Legislative Risk	Diversification
Reinvestment Risk	Long Maturities, Diversification
Opportunity Cost	Diversification

From the above table, you might conclude that we love diversification. We do.

Rewards of Bond Investing

With all these risks at play in bond investing, there must be rewards to offset them. Otherwise, no one would buy bonds.

There *is* reward indeed. The return you get can be thought of as payment precisely for assuming the risks outlined above. Bonds can give you a large and stable rate of return on your money. Putting your capital to play in the bond market is an efficient and effective way to lock in a given rate of return with a high likelihood of getting your money back in the end. With your wealth capitalized in bonds, you convert it into a predictable stream of payments around which you can plan your life (and do so without dipping into principal). In addition, the income you receive as a bond investor is often higher than what you could get from a CD or passbook savings account.

Once you've decided to own bonds, how do you maximize your income from them? Academic researchers who have studied the returns from fixed-income investing find that two factors have generally determined outcomes. Investors have sought greater total returns by purchasing bonds that are *longer in maturity* and *lower in credit quality*. But how have these strategies worked?

Maturity

Figure 4.1 shows some of the rewards (the annual returns) and risks (the standard deviations) of bond investing from 1926 to 2002. *Standard deviation* is a statistical measure of how much a value varies from its average. The higher the standard deviation, the more it fluctuates, and so, it is believed, the higher the risk. Consider this: Even though government bonds have virtually no default risk, their prices can and do go up and down according to the interest rate environment surrounding them.

Figure 4.1: Risks vs. Returns of Bond Investing 1926–2002

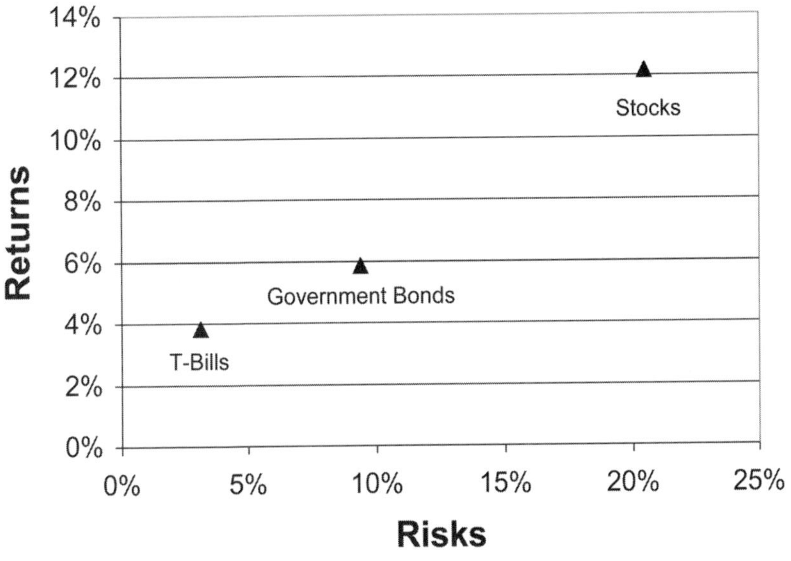

In each case above, we've plotted the return (on the vertical axis, where higher is better) against the risks (the standard deviation on the horizontal axis, where closer to the vertical axis is better). You can see that one-month Treasury bills have the lowest average annual return (3.8 percent) and the lowest risk (3.2 percent).

Next, you'll see that long-term bonds have about 50 percent more total annual return, but at a price of three times the total risk. Stocks have much higher risks and returns than either T-bills or bonds.

Here's the moral from Figure 4.1: *The premium investors have received for taking the added maturity risk of long-term bonds compared to short-term Treasury bills has historically been outweighed by the added risk they assumed.* As a follow-up, Table 4.2 shows how going longer in maturity on Treasury securities affected our risks (standard deviation) from 1964 to 2001 without any commensurate improvement in annualized returns:

Table 4.2: Rewards/Risks of Treasury Maturities 1964–2001				
Maturity:	**1 Month**	**1 Year**	**5 Years**	**20 Years**
Reward	6.40%	7.10%	7.70%	7.50%
Risk	1.20%	2.40%	6.30%	11.10%

During the debilitating rise in interest rates from 1946 to 1981, long-term government-bond yields rose from 1.9 percent to 15 percent. Bond prices were in free-fall, and long-term government bonds returned an average of *minus* 2.5 percent annually after inflation over the entire 36-year period. No wonder T-bills look so attractive by comparison.

Credit Quality

Figure 4.2 compares the risks and returns of the Lehman Brothers Government Bond Index with the slightly lower credit quality of the Lehman Brothers Corporate Bond Index from 1986 to 1998.

Figure 4.2: Rewards and Risks by Credit Quality 1986–1998

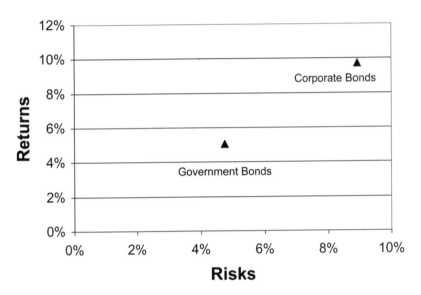

Not surprisingly, the corporate bonds have higher returns, and, as you might expect, slightly higher risks (that is, their values fluctuate more than those of the government bonds). Keep in mind that in the real world, transaction costs impinge upon the "pure" performance of the corporate bonds portrayed in the index. While government bonds can be bought directly from the government without additional fees, the buying and selling of corporate bonds entails commissions that subtract directly from their returns—but not from their risks. This would hold especially true for a buyer of individual corporate bonds, who couldn't be expected to get the price breaks offered to a major mutual fund. Adding this expense back in, it looks as if holding corporate bonds over this period added about 0.6 percent in annual returns, at the price of about 0.3 percent increase in annual price fluctuation—a trade-off that we think is worth making. On the other hand, the period under consideration (1986 to 1998) is relatively short. Unfortunately, historians of finance have not reached a consensus about the returns and risks of corporate bonds for the earlier part of the 20th century.

Thank you for bearing with us through this bond primer. Now we'll move on to some specifics for the income-oriented investor.

CHAPTER FIVE

Essential Bonds for Fixed-Income Investors

In light of the risks and rewards we've described so far, we think that there are certain categories of bonds that have a place in your portfolio. We're going to present these in order of increasing risk—which also means in order of increasing yield—over the next two chapters. The bonds in this chapter are lower in yield, but they need to be considered for a significant portion of your fixed-income holdings. Then in Chapter 6, we'll look at some that are a bit dicier, with higher yields (and risks) to match.

Ultra-Short Bonds

Conservative investors love the safety of instruments like passbook savings accounts and money market funds that promise 100 cents for each dollar invested. However, they pay a price for a fixed $1 net asset value, and that price is a low yield. When everyone cleaves to this absolute stability, it sets up a disproportionate reward for being willing to accept slightly more risk.

The typical money market fund does not contain money at all. It takes your cash and buys government and corporate loans with an average maturity of about 90 days. But what if you were willing to extend the maturity to 180 days? While the price of your bonds could vary slightly, you might be repaid with an extra percentage point in yield. If you're willing to accept a little more risk, adding some ultra-short-term corporate bonds to the government bonds, you could get a still higher yield.

We don't mean to downplay the added risk, since if there weren't any, ultra-short bond funds would pay no more than money market funds. Still, we think this risk is worth taking. To the yield-starved investor of today, getting an extra percentage point or two of interest is like manna from heaven.

Keep the money you need for immediate expenses in the form of cash in a checking account or money market fund (you can find one with a good rate at **www.bankrate.com** or **www.ibcdata.com**). The short answer (as of today) is to open a money market account at Vanguard (**www.vanguard.com**) or link your bank's checking account to the FDIC-insured money market fund over the Internet at **www.ingdirect.com.** We like these options better than short-term Certificates of Deposit, even including the new bump-up CDs and step-up CDs, for the rising interest-rate environment investors face at present.

Then, put the rest of the money you otherwise would have kept in cash in ultra-short bonds; Table 5.1 gives some examples. Be aware that our table shows trailing 12-month yields, while your money market fund may report a 30-day (or even 7-day) yield, making a head-to-head comparison difficult. In a rising-interest-rate environment, money market funds may even do better than ultra-short-term bond funds, as they can turn over their short-term paper more quickly. In a falling- or stable-interest-rate environment, the ultra-short bond fund should do better by opting for slightly longer maturities and casting off from the $1-per-share net-asset value.

Table 5.1: Ultra-Short Bond Funds 09/2004					
Name	**Ticker**	**Yield**	**Maturity**	**Credit**	**Expense**
Schwab Yield Plus	SWYPX	2.5%	2.7 yrs	A	0.56%
Fidelity Ultra Short Bond	FUSFX	1.2%	1.8 yrs	A	0.55%
Constellation CIP UltraShort	TSDOX	2.1%	1.4 yrs	AAA	0.41%
Payden Limited Maturity	PYLMX	1.5%	1.2 yrs	AAA	0.40%

Corporate Money Market Funds

Another way that you can get a better yield while still keeping a nominal $1-per-share price is by using a corporate money market fund. While ultra-short bond funds gain an edge by taking a step out in maturity, these funds pay a higher yield by taking on single-company business risk, forgoing the diversification that most money market and ultra-short-term bond funds offer. As of this writing, four companies offer their own in-house money market funds, and the number may grow.

Started as a perk for employees, these accounts are really a source of cheap financing for the companies that sponsor them. Why should they go through the expensive intermediary of the capital markets to raise money if investors are willing to beat a path directly to their doors?

These four companies are Caterpillar, General Electric, General Motor's GMAC Bank, and Ford—you may have heard of them. They all have substantial credit departments and, as Table 5.2 shows, the yields paid by their in-house money market funds surpass those available elsewhere.

Table 5.2 Corporate Money Market Funds 09/2004			
Company	**Yield**	**Minimum**	**Phone No.**
Caterpillar	1.5–2%	$250	(800) 504-1114
General Electric	1.8–2.3%	$500	(800) 433-4480
Ford	2.1–2.4%	$1,000	(800) 580-4778
GMAC Bank	2–2.1%	$500	(866) 246-2265

The usual rules for money market funds still apply. You can write checks against your account, but small ones (below $250) will trigger a special charge, as will accounts that fall below a minimum balance.

There's just one problem: risk. What if Ford or Caterpillar declares bankruptcy? If you think that can't happen, talk to some Kmart stockholders. American car manufacturers haven't exactly been rolling in dough lately, and there's little evidence that the situation is improving, despite the handwriting having been on the wall since, oh, 1970. Workers at these companies should definitely park their money elsewhere: Imagine losing your job and your savings on the same day.

Losing your savings? If these companies fail, you'll line up with other bondholders to get your money back. Okay, so you may not lose everything, but what if you lose 70 cents on the dollar, and you have to wait a few years to get it back? The risk of extending maturity via the ultra-short bond funds is often worth taking, since the potential for loss is both small and finite. Here, the risk is small but potentially catastrophic. This is your *cash* we're talking about— the portion of your assets that you presumably want to expose to the least amount of risk.

If you find the temptation overwhelming, please put only a portion of your money into one of these companies. Since the yield implicitly reflects the credit rating, we'd favor choosing the one with the lowest yield rather than the highest—the opposite of what your instincts might tell you. General Electric has AAA credit, and it's worth sacrificing a little yield to get it. But GMAC Bank goes one step further and offers FDIC insurance on money market accounts up to $100,000, making it the winner in this category.

Short-Term Bonds

As long as you've started down the slope from the engraved U.S. dollar, why not go one step further? You could assemble a fund of short-term bonds ranging from one to five years in maturity and get an even higher yield. Depending on the credit quality you seek

(Treasury notes? Federal paper? Corporate bonds?), here are some yields currently available on some low-expense, no-load, short-term bond funds:

Table 5.3: Short-Term Bond Fund Yields 09/2004

Fund	Ticker	Yield	Maturity	Credit	Expense
Constellation CIP Short Dur. Fixed Inc.	TSDGX	2.7%	2.1 yrs	AAA	0.40%
Fidelity Short-Term Bond	FSHBX	2.4%	2.4 yrs	AA	0.57%
Harbor Short Duration	HASDX	3.2%	1.6 yrs	AAA	0.36%
Payden Short Bond Fund	PYSBX	1.9%	2.1 yrs	AAA	0.50%
Schwab Short-Term Bond	SWBDX	2.7%	3.2 yrs	AAA	0.43%
TIAA-CREF Short-Term Bond	TCSTX	2.8%	2.5 yrs	AAA	0.30%
USAA Short-Term Bond	USSBX	3.2%	1.8 yrs	AA	0.55%
iShares Lehman 1–3 Year Treasury	SHY	1.8%	1.7 yrs	AAA	0.15%
Vanguard Short-Term Treasury Bond	VFISX	2.6%	1.9 yrs	AAA	0.26%
Vanguard Short-Term Bond Index	VBISX	2.9%	2.7 yrs	AAA	0.20%
Vanguard Short-Term Inv. Grade Bond	VFSTX	3.5%	2.4 yrs	AA	0.21%

We've already seen that the bear market in long-term bonds over most of the 20th century has made short-term, high-quality bonds the place to be—the most reward for the least risk. Accordingly, these short-term bonds should occupy a position of honor within your portfolio.

A five-year ladder of individual Treasury notes would be a useful alternative to consider, having an average maturity of two to three years, and a 0.00 percent expense ratio (if set up at **www. treasurydirect.gov**), and perfect credit. Treasury Direct does charge a $25 annual fee on accounts larger than $100,000, but extremely frugal investors have been known to circumvent even this small fee by simply opening more than one account.

Inflation-Indexed Treasuries (TIPS)

The U.S. government began issuing Treasury Inflation-Protected Securities in 1997. These are going to be important to your portfolio, and so are worth pausing to consider.

Most paper assets—like stocks and bonds—are ravaged by inflation, but TIPS aren't. More than any other paper asset, they are immune from purchasing-power risk, which effectively makes them a new asset class for investors. If inflation hits and your stocks and bonds tank, TIPS will appreciate (or at least maintain their real value). If deflation hits, you'll still have locked in a reasonable rate of return from a payer—Uncle Sam—who's going to meet his obligations no matter what, and who promises to never return less than original par value at maturity. TIPS protect you either way.

No wonder some financial advisors recommend that the entire bond position of a portfolio consist of nothing but these inflation-linked securities. While prices of long-maturity bonds fluctuate wildly with changes in interest rates, long-maturity-dated TIPS act like shorter-maturity bonds due to their inflation-protection shield, and this makes them a fairly conservative investment.

Their recent popularity shouldn't mask the fact that their prices *will* fluctuate, which means that they can go down as well as up. In recent years, the total returns from owning TIPS have made them a win-win proposition. Investors have gotten free inflation protection and a stock-market-beating return in the bargain.

The mechanism underlying how TIPS work is more complicated than that of regular Treasury bonds. If you own an ordinary $1,000 par value 20-year Treasury bond yielding 5 percent, then every year for 20 years you'd receive $50 in interest (paid out in two $25 installments), and two decades later you'd get your $1,000 returned. If you own an inflation-indexed Treasury bond yielding 5 percent, and inflation were 3 percent the first year, the Treasury would assume the bond was worth $1,030 by the year's end ($1,000 par value plus $30 to compensate for the 3 percent inflation). Additionally, your interest payment would be adjusted for inflation as well (to oversimplify slightly, it would be 5 percent of $1,030, or $51.50, instead of the $50 you would have received from a non-inflation-linked Treasury bond). This benefit isn't free. To compensate for it, yields on inflation-indexed securities are lower than those on conventional Treasuries.

The principal that is returned to you when the bond matures is adjusted for inflation. But in order to make your life as complicated as possible, *the government will tax you on each yearly increase in principal, even though you won't receive the actual money until the bond matures.* This creates what's known as *phantom income*, but the IRS wants to be paid in genuine dollars. Take an extreme example: Inflation hits 100 percent. You own $100,000 worth of these inflation-indexed securities, so inflation adds $100,000 to the value of your TIPS this year, and you're in the 35 percent tax bracket. The government wants $35,000 in taxes from you on the phantom income this year, even though you won't actually receive the money until the bonds mature in, say, 20 years. Because of scenarios like this, it's wisest to keep TIPS in tax-deferred accounts like IRAs and Keoghs.

I Bonds

If you don't have any room left in your tax-sheltered accounts, you can buy inflation-linked Series I Savings Bonds from **www.treasurydirect.gov.** The advantage with the Series I bonds is that, unlike with the TIPS, your income isn't taxed until you're actually paid upon redemption. However, other restrictions apply.

I Bonds are sold at face value, in denominations ranging from $50 to $10,000. The interest accrues as long as you own them, and you're paid (along with the return of your principal, both adjusted semiannually by the rate of inflation) when you sell them. *This means that I Bonds are somewhat impractical for income investors, since you don't realize the income until they are sold.*

You can buy (and redeem) I Bonds from any local bank or financial institution where U.S. Savings Bonds are sold, or directly from the Treasury at the government Website mentioned above, with a maximum purchase amount of $30,000 per year from each place.

As of September 2004, the coupon rate on I Bonds is 1.0 percent (the rate that's then adjusted by the rate of inflation), and you can hold them for up to 30 years. Rates are reset every six months. Like other federal government bonds, I Bonds are free of state and local taxes. You must hold them for at least one year, and if you cash them in within five years, the government will subtract three months' interest as a penalty. This penalty also makes them impractical for building short-term bond ladders. In fact, they're mentioned here for completeness, since they aren't really suitable for income at all.

A Catch

Before you rush off to the Treasury Department to convert your life savings into TIPS, there's this to consider: Who decides what the rate of inflation is? Answer: the federal government—the same folks who are going to be repaying the loan. Since the government acts as both payee and umpire, this creates a moral hazard. The inflation quotient is determined by the Consumer Price Index for All Urban Consumers (CPI-U), an index managed by the Bureau of Labor Statistics. If the bureaucrats at the Department of the Treasury ever sit down over cigars and brandy with the bureaucrats at the Department of Labor, who knows what kind of adjustment for inflation might be made? We're not talking exact science here, like space shuttle launches. The CPI is "smoothed" to avoid large jumps, it is managed to take advantage of what economists call *substitution effects*, and *hedonic adjustments* are increasingly built into most of its components (to reflect improvements in quality, ha-ha).

While economists estimate that historically the CPI has actually overstated inflation by as much as one percent per year, now, with these changes afoot, it's probably *under*stating inflation by a like amount. What will it do in the future? Who knows? Too many people are affected by the CPI for it to completely disconnect from reality, but the fact that government economists are always monkeying with it subjects TIPS to *revision risk*.

Because TIPS compete head-to-head with Treasury bonds, you can instantly deduce the market's expectation of inflation by subtracting the TIPS yield from the nominal (that is, non-inflation indexed) Treasury bond yield of the same maturity. Let's do the math: As of September 2004, nominal ten-year Treasury bonds are yielding 4.18 percent, while ten-year TIPS yield 1.82 percent. This implies that, other things being equal, the expected rate of inflation is 2.36 percent (4.18 minus 1.82) annually over the next ten years.

What are you to make of this nugget of wisdom? Figure 5.1 shows how this forward-looking market estimate of inflation compares with historical experience of the last 10 and 25 years.

Figure 5.1: TIPS vs. Nominal Treasury Yields 09/2004

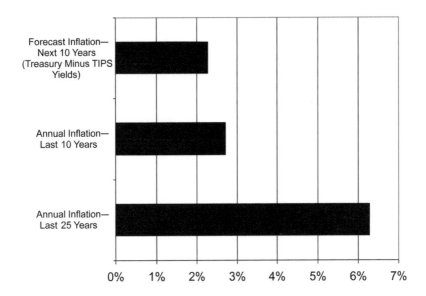

At worst, the anticipated inflation priced into TIPS over the next decade is close to the rate of inflation that's been simmering over the past decade. It's significantly less than that which prevailed over the last quarter century.

The downside of TIPS is their low yield. It kills us to recommend them to high income oriented investors, but we feel duty-bound to warn you of the dangers of leaving home without them. Considering the long-term inflationary pressures at work in the economy, and how politically expedient a major bout of inflation will be in helping the government solve its looming debt crisis at some future date, we see a great deal of wisdom in stocking up.

How to Buy TIPS

Perhaps the easiest way to buy TIPS for tax-deferred accounts is through the intermediary of a no-load, low-expense mutual fund. Table 5.4 rounds up the usual suspects for your shopping pleasure.

Table 5.4: TIPS Funds 09/2004			
Fund	Ticker	Yield	Expense
American Century Inflation Bond	ACITX	4.2%	0.50%
Fidelity Inflation-Protected Securities	FINPX	1.4%	0.50%
iShares Inflation-Protected Securities	TIP	4.9%*	0.20%
TIAA-CREF Inflation-Linked Bond	TCILX	3.8%	0.30%
T Rowe Price Inflation-Protected	PRIPX	1.4%	0.50%
Vanguard Inflation-Protected Securities	VIPSX	4.4%	0.18%

* Current Yield, not Trailing 12-Month Yield

Even more briefly (than what we just presented in Table 5.4), the choice is between Vanguard and iShares, because of their low expense ratios. Vanguard is an open-end mutual fund, while iShares is a closed-end exchange-traded fund (much more about the difference between these two types of mutual funds in a moment). It really comes down to which is administratively more convenient. Alternately, you have the option of buying TIPS directly from the government at **www.treasurydirect.gov.**

Agency Bonds

Here are some of the various agencies of the U.S. government (and groups historically associated with it) that love borrowing money to spend on your behalf.

GNMA Mortgage Bonds

The Government National Mortgage Association (Ginnie Mae or GNMA) is an agency of the federal government created in 1968 to help finance government-assisted housing programs. Its function is to buy mortgages, pool them, and then sell $25,000 "pass-through" certificates representing an interest in the pool. Unlike the pass-through certificates issued by its sister agencies (Freddie Mac and Fannie Mae), the Ginnie Mae bonds have been transmuted by Congress to explicitly carry the full faith and credit of the U.S. government. Even if every mortgage holder in the pool defaults, the government promises to make good on the bonds.

There's not a lot to like about mortgage bonds. Human nature being what it is, when mortgage rates are low, people refinance, and your high-yielding mortgage bond disappears. When rates go up, folks sit on their low mortgages and refuse to refinance, denying you the higher rate you'd like. So what's the deal? Why do we mention them?

Here's the reason: As Table 5.5 shows, GNMA bonds yield a percentage point or two over comparable Treasuries, yet still carry the U.S. government "Good Housekeeping" guarantee. But be warned: When interests rate fall and massive refinancing takes place, your income will fall and so will the desirability of owning GNMAs. And unlike Treasury bonds, the interest on GNMA notes is taxable at the state and local level. But when interest rates rise or stand pat (so there's no special inducement to refinance), you collect the benefit of the extra yield.

Table 5.5: GNMA Bond Funds 09/2004				
Fund	**Ticker**	**Yield**	**Maturity**	**Expense**
Fidelity GNMA	FGMNX	3.6%	3.8 yrs	0.57%
Payden GNMA	PYGNX	6.1%	5.1 yrs	0.50%
T. Rowe Price GNMA	PRGMX	4.3%	5.7 yrs	0.69%
USAA GNMA	USGNX	4.8%	4.2 yrs	0.47%
Vanguard GNMA	VFIIX	4.7%	5.8 yrs	0.20%

One useful feature of mortgage bonds is that, unlike other government and corporate bonds, GNMA bonds make their payments monthly (as people make their mortgage payments). Along with the interest comes a return of principal, since mortgage loans are amortized and a portion of principal is returned each month as well, as is the principal from any prepayments. This portion of your monthly check isn't taxable, and the fund tells you how much of each kind of income you received in your tax statement at year's end.

NEXT, WE'LL LOOK AT EIGHT MORE government-associated enterprises that go beyond the GNMA.

Fannie Mae and Freddie Mac

The Federal National Mortgage Association ("Fannie Mae") was created in 1968 and the Federal Home Loan Mortgage Corporation in 1970 ("Freddie Mac"), ostensibly to fund mortgages for low-income people, but with the effect of subsidizing the housing market at the expense of other sectors of the American economy. These are by far the largest players in the $7 trillion mortgage market, since their implicit government backing allows them to borrow money on favorable terms unavailable to competitors. Notwithstanding their federal charters, they have since been privatized, and their stocks trade on the New York Stock Exchange. While most federal-agency debt is tax-exempt at the state and local levels, income from these privatized agency obligations is fully taxable across the board.

These entities sell bonds and use the money to purchase mortgages in the secondary market. The mortgages are then "securitized" into various kinds of pass-through instruments and resold. Since investors believe that these agencies are too big to fail, their bonds are rated AAA, despite the inscrutability of their financial statements, their heavy use of derivatives, and the lack of meaningful oversight. It's unclear whether anyone really understands what's going on with Fannie Mae's and Freddie Mac's bond portfolios, yet the failure of these agencies would have far-reaching implications.

If the unhappy day ever arrives when they come crashing down, the government will probably step up to the plate and bail them out with our tax dollars. Meanwhile, these powerful groups are ever on the alert for ways to expand their missions. One recent headline said that Fannie Mae wants to start a joint-venture company to spur the nascent Egyptian mortgage market (no, we're not making this up).

As we write this, Fannie Mae's books are being subjected to an unprecedented level of examination by its overseer. How this will shake out is anyone's guess, but it may not be pretty.

Federal Home Loan Banks

Created in 1932, the Federal Home Loan (FHL) Banks issue loans to savings and loan institutions (S&Ls) through $10,000 non-callable bonds. At the time it was founded, the idea was to shore up these banks during the Great Depression. The private market hadn't found it profitable to issue home-mortgage loans longer than five years, but once the risk was transferred from the banks to the government, the S&Ls felt confident in issuing far longer-term loans, and the 30-year mortgage was invented.

In recent decades, Americans have withdrawn their assets from these institutions and put them into various kinds of money market and mutual funds. Deprived of the capital that these deposits represented and having no money to lend out, the S&Ls, community banks, and credit unions would have had difficulty staying in business. The FHL Banks came to their rescue, advancing the cash they needed to stay afloat. Instead of having to borrow from depositors at market rates, these institutions now get their money straight from the FHL Banks at rates set not by the market, but by government regulators. Not surprisingly, the banks' mission has expanded to making all manner of local business and agricultural loans. These bonds are rated AAA and have an implicit backing by the government (which may or may not turn out to be the same as *actual* backing by the government).

DESPITE THE BILLIONS OF DOLLARS that these privatized federal mortgage agencies receive in the form of taxpayer subsidies, a scant 2 percent goes to helping Americans earning below-median incomes realize the dream of home ownership. Minorities are actually underrepresented within the group served, according to watchdog group **www.fmpolicyfocus.org.** Yet go to their Websites, and there's nothing but smiling minority faces, implying that they're just out to do good by helping people in need. This is the fig leaf under which they do business.

The uncertainty regarding these agencies means that we aren't big fans of their investment opportunities. We prefer GNMA bonds, where the government backing is explicit, and we think it's worth the small premium (in the form of a reduced yield) to get it. However, many reasonable people disagree, so Table 5.6 shows two funds that invest in mortgage-backed securities. There are also private (that is, entirely nongovernmental) companies that sell collateralized mortgage obligations, and these may also be represented to some extent in the holdings of these mutual funds.

Table 5.6: Mortgage Security Funds 09/2004				
Fund	Ticker	Yield	Maturity	Expense
Dreyfus U.S. Mortgage Securities	DIGFX	4.6%	8.3 yrs	0.68%
Fidelity Mortgage Securities	FMSFX	3.1%	3.5 yrs	0.60%

Federal Farm Credit System

In 1916, Congress established the Federal Farm Credit System to make sure that funding would be available to farmers. It includes the Federal Land Banks, the Federal Intermediate Credit Banks, and the Banks for Cooperatives. As with most government programs, this one has had a number of perverse economic effects.

As James Bovard writes in a Cato Institute study: "By flooding America's least competent farmers with easy credit and bailouts, Congress and FmHA [Farmers Home Administration] have spurred a boom-bust cycle in farmland values, helped bankrupt many farmers, imposed huge entry barriers on young farmers, and driven up the cost of crop production, thereby undercutting U.S. exports. With each federal farm credit disaster, the government's dominance over agricultural credit has increased; FmHA and the Farm Credit System now effectively control half of the nation's farm debt."

As of this writing, they have $93 billion worth of debt outstanding. They do have an AAA rating but no explicit backing by the Federal government—although the government did bail them out in 1987, forever imprinting the idea in investors' minds that these government agency bonds would surely be rescued from default by the generosity of the nation's taxpayers.

We'll discuss how to buy these (and the agency bonds that follow) in a moment. But first, let's continue our tour of government agencies in action.

Sallie Mae

The Student Loan Marketing Association, or Sallie Mae, was founded in 1973 and privatized in 1977. It purchases student loans from colleges and banks, and then sells debentures backed by these loans. Their bonds are all rated AAA because of the implicit U.S. government backing, and the income from them is taxable at all levels.

Resolution Trust Corporation

The Resolution Trust Corporation was created in 1989 to replace the Federal Savings and Loan Insurance Corporation and bail out the 750 savings and loan associations that collapsed in part as a result of the junk-bond fiasco. As receiver, it sold assets of failed S&Ls and paid insured depositors. In 1995, its duties, including insurance of deposits in thrift institutions, were transferred to the Savings Association Insurance Fund. It no longer issues new bonds, but its existing bonds continue to be serviced.

Federal Housing Administration

The Federal Housing Administration was created in 1934 during the Great Depression to insure long-term mortgages, thereby making home ownership (and a stake in our capitalist society) affordable by the masses. If the mortgage holder defaulted, the government promised to step in and keep up the payments. Since the FHA's preferred model of home ownership was a detached single-family residence in a zoned neighborhood, the net effect was to encircle America's cities with white suburbs, since few other groups qualified for the government guarantees. As a result, banks redlined the inner cities as unacceptable places to lend money, and these neighborhoods crumbled (except for those inhabited by the wealthy, who never needed the loan guarantees in the first place). While the mission of the FHA is to build healthy neighborhoods and communities, sometimes unscrupulous banks, Realtors, and appraisers have conspired to take advantage of the FHA guarantee such that now the agency is the single largest owner of vacant properties in the country (45,000 in 2001) and engages in tens of thousands of foreclosures per year. The FHA no longer issues loans directly, but existing loans are rated AAA and are free of state and local taxes.

Tennessee Valley Authority

In 1933, President Roosevelt asked Congress to create "a corporation clothed with the power of government but possessed of the flexibility and initiative of a private enterprise," and as a result, the Tennessee Valley Authority was launched to provide for the integrated development of the Tennessee River basin. It became a government-run electric utility, and issued bonds backed with the full faith and credit of the government to build new power plants. It no longer issues bonds and has become self-financing—for now, anyway.

How to Buy Agency Bonds

Since you can buy Treasury bonds with no commission directly from the government by going to **www.treasurydirect.gov,** the advantage in yield of owning these government-agency bonds (privatized or otherwise) is directly reduced by the necessity of purchasing them through brokers who will charge you a commission (visible or invisible) for their trouble. This puts you at a disadvantage compared to institutional customers who may be buying tens of millions of dollars' worth of the same bonds. Since you can't beat them, the next best thing is to join them, by buying these bonds through a no-load, low-expense mutual fund.

For example, Vanguard's Short-Term Federal Bond fund (ticker: VSGBX) is full of government paper, taking a step down from the pristine credit quality of U.S. Treasury bonds found in their Short-Term Treasury Bond Fund (ticker: VFISX), and for the very small amount of added credit risk, you get about 18 basis points (one basis point = 1/100th of a percentage point) in yield over their pure Treasury fund.

Table 5.7: Short-Term Government Bond Funds

Fund	Ticker	Yield	Maturity	Expense
Excelsior Short-Term Government	UMGVX	2.8%	2.5 yrs	0.53%
Payden U.S. Government	PYUSX	2.3%	2.8 yrs	0.45%
Vanguard Short-Term Federal	VSGBX	2.8%	2.1 yrs	0.22%

On the other hand, you'll get a higher yield if you take one more step down in credit quality to . . .

Investment-Grade Corporate Bonds

Corporate bonds rated "Aaa" by Moody's or "AAA" by Standard & Poor's are judged to be of the highest investment quality and considered to be "gilt edged." Interest payments are protected by a comfortable margin within the issuers' cash flows and the principal is considered to be quite secure.

Companies whose debt merited the AAA rating in October 2004 were few, and included the likes of General Electric, Pfizer, Merck, and Mobil Oil. A month later, a little bout of Vioxx happened to Merck, knocking its credit rating down two notches (to "A" credit) in the matter of a day. Let this be a lesson to us all.

The vast majority of these bonds come from the agencies we just discussed, like Fannie Mae and Freddie Mac. In these cases, the AAA ratings are not due to the financial scrupulousness with which these institutions conduct their businesses and their rock-solid balance sheets, but rather because Moody's and Standard & Poor's believe that taxpayers would be forced to bail them out should massive defaults occur.

For taking this added measure of credit risk beyond pure U.S. Treasury notes, investors are rewarded with a higher yield. As of this writing, AAA bonds are yielding about 5.5 percent annually, compared with a yield of 4.8 percent for treasury bonds of similar maturity. The availability of higher yields holds true across the spectrum of maturities, and it gets progressively higher as you descend through the ranks of investment-grade corporate bonds (Standard & Poor's "BBB" or Moody's "Baa" being the lowest investment-grade rating).

Table 5.8 lists the 30 companies that comprise the Dow Jones Industrial Average, along with their current S&P Credit Ratings— loosely, the expert opinion as to their ability to repay debt, with AAA being the highest and BBB the lowest in this table.

Table 5.8: Credit Ratings of the DJ Industrials 09/2004

Dow Component	S&P Credit Rating
3M	AA
Alcoa	A
Altria	BBB
American Express	A
American International Group	AAA
Boeing	A
Caterpillar	A
Citigroup	AA
Coca-Cola	A
DuPont	AA
Exxon Mobil	AAA
General Electric	AAA
General Motors	BBB
Hewlett-Packard	A
Home Depot	AA
Honeywell	A
Intel	A
IBM	A
JPMorgan Chase	A
Johnson & Johnson	AAA
McDonald's	A
Merck	AAA*
Microsoft	AA
Pfizer	AAA
Procter & Gamble	AA
SBC Communications	A
United Technologies	A
Verizon	A
Wal-Mart	AA
Walt Disney	BBB

* "A" as of 11/2004

Here are 30 of the greatest companies in the world, yet only three of them merit the highest AAA credit rating. Three of them have the *lowest* possible investment grade credit rating—BBB—one notch above "junk" status.

Expand this list to the elite companies in the S&P 500, and you'll find that until fairly recently only 12 of the 500 (less than 3 percent) had AAA status, while fully 25 percent were considered "junk."

Our point is simply this: Many perfectly fine companies do not make the AAA credit quality list, so if you're willing to take the risk of owning these companies by buying their stocks, it might be worthwhile to own their bonds as well.

As Figure 5.2 shows, you obtain greater total returns buying investment-grade corporate bonds with a lower credit rating than AAA—but you do so at the price of greater risk. The returns here are all from Lehman Brothers bond indexes.

Figure 5.2: Corporate Bond Risks vs. Returns 1986–1998

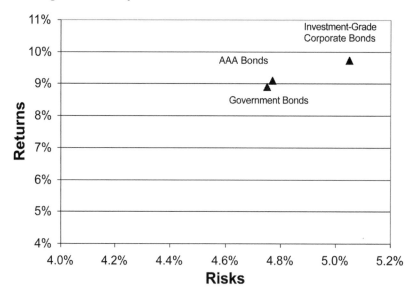

Risk here is again defined as annual standard deviation (a measure of how much their prices go up and down) and not risk of default—

which would be zero for U.S. government bonds. Intermediate-term investment-grade corporate bonds take two giant steps away from the riskless T-bill: They take a step out in maturity, from 90 days to anywhere from 5 to 12 years, and a step down in credit quality, from government/AAA credit quality ranging down to a Standard & Poor's BBB or a Moody's Baa rating. The extent of the advantage they offer over riskless Treasury bonds changes with the shape of the credit and yield curves. In today's low-interest-rate environment, going to intermediate-term corporate bonds extracts an extra third of a percentage point in yield.

While individual investors can purchase U.S. Treasury bonds directly from Uncle Sam, once you head into corporate territory, you push off from the happy shore of transaction-free trading. The answer to these fees is to buy corporate bonds through the vehicle of a no-load, low-expense mutual fund and let the fund manager use the economies of scale to get the bonds at reasonable prices. Table 5.9 offers some high-quality, intermediate-term bond funds for your consideration, listed in order of decreasing credit quality.

Table 5.9: Investment-Grade Intermediate-Term Bond Funds 09/2004					
Fund	**Ticker**	**Yield**	**Maturity**	**Credit**	**Expense**
Dodge & Cox Income	DODIX	4.4%	5.6 yrs	AA	0.45%
Fidelity Intermediate Bond	FTHRX	3.4%	4.3 yrs	AA	0.61%
iShares Lehman Brothers Aggregate	AGG	3.7%*	5.9 yrs	AA	0.20%
Schwab Total Bond Market Index	SWLBX	3.1%	9.0 yrs	AA	0.43%
TIAA-CREF Bond Plus	TIPBX	3.7%	6.4 yrs	AAA	0.30%
T. Rowe Price US Bond Index	PBDIX	4.1%	7.1 yrs	AAA	0.30%
USAA Income	USAIX	4.5%	6.1 yrs	AA	0.50%
Vanguard Int.-Term Inv. Grade Bond	VFICX	4.7%	6.0 yrs	A	0.20%
Vanguard Int.-Term Bond Index	VBIIX	4.7%	7.6 yrs	AA	0.20%
Vanguard Int.-Term Treasury	VFITX	4.4%	6.0 yrs	AAA	0.26%
Vanguard Total Bond Market Index	VBMFX	4.4%	7.7 yrs	AAA	0.22%

* Current Yield, not Trailing 12-Month Yield

The Vanguard Intermediate-Term Treasury Fund (fees are 0.28 percent per annually) would be an alternative to holding a ten-year Treasury bond ladder. You could do something similar on your own by buying Treasury notes of two-, four-, six-, eight-, and ten-year maturities in a bond ladder as well. You'd have an average maturity of four to six years, perfect credit quality, and zero management expenses beyond your own time to set up and maintain the account. That said, by adding agency and corporate debt, your yields will increase.

A number of the funds above (VBMFX, AGG, PBDIX, and SWLBX) are based on something called the Lehman Brothers Aggregate Bond Index. This is the bogey that every fixed-income manager in the country tries to beat, in much the same way as the S&P 500 Index serves as the stock market benchmark by which equity managers pace themselves. The Lehman Brothers are to bonds what the Smith Brothers are to cough drops.

The Lehman Aggregate Index attempts to replicate the performance of a portfolio holding every publicly traded investment-grade bond in the United States: short-, intermediate-, and long-term; treasury; corporate; agency; mortgage; and even international dollar-denominated bonds. It throws in everything but the kitchen sink—only junk bonds are excluded. While you can't invest in the index directly, investment companies have licensed the index and offer bond mutual funds that track it, like Vanguard's Total Bond Market Index (VBMFX) and Barclay's iShares Lehman Aggregate Bond (AGG). This is the one-stop, no-brain, set-it-and-forget-it decision for people who don't want to delve further into the complexities of the bond market. The index has a trailing 12-month yield of 4.4 percent as of this writing.

Corporate Inflation-Linked Notes

The newest kids on the inflation-protected bond block are corporate inflation-linked notes. Seeing how hugely successful the government's TIPS offerings were, it was only natural that corporate America would want to get into the act, but there are some significant differences between the two types of bonds that are worth underscoring.

Foremost is credit risk. While the U.S. government is famous for paying its bills, corporate bonds involve some degree of credit risk. So far, the issuers include Merrill Lynch, Morgan Stanley, and John Hancock Life Insurance (now owned by Manulife)—large, well-capitalized companies with good credit ratings—but there's still a gap between even the best corporate credit and that of the U.S. government.

Then there's taxation. Government bonds aren't taxed at the state and local level, while corporate bondholders find every type of tax collector reaching into their pockets. There's also an important area where corporate inflation-linked bonds have an edge. As we mentioned, the government will want to tax you every year on your phantom income from TIPS—income that's recorded on paper this year but won't really be paid out in cash until the bond matures. But their corporate counterparts adjust their coupons by the Consumer Price Index every payday. If inflation hits in a big way, you'll have the requisite cash on hand to pay your tax bills. This makes the corporate inflation-linked notes suitable for taxable accounts in a way that TIPS are not.

Since they actually pay out the inflation portion of their coupons, corporate inflation-indexed notes are friendlier to income investors looking for a cash flow to cover current expenses. Another attractive feature, at least for some income investors, is that coupons are paid on a monthly basis, not semiannually, as with TIPS.

There's one more thing we like about them: The maturities of these notes are five, seven, and ten years: significantly shorter than those of the Treasury inflation-indexed bonds.

Now the bad news: These securities are so new that no one has yet created a low-expense mutual fund that contains a diversified portfolio of them (to reduce credit risk). Such a fund could use its purchasing power to buy them at a price that places the small-fry individual retail investor on an equal footing with institutional clients. We have no doubt that such an investment vehicle will materialize sooner or later—perhaps even by the time you read this. Check our Website, and we'll let you know.

When this day comes, these inflation-indexed bonds will be a worthy addition to your fixed-income portfolios.

Repackaged Corporate Bonds

Over the past few years, in an attempt to "sex up" corporate bonds for ordinary investors, various brokerage houses have purchased large blocks of individual securities (at $1,000 par) and then broken them up into bite-sized pieces that trade at $25 par. These are essentially pass-through securities, traded under confusing proprietary names given to them by the brokerage houses that do the slicing and dicing, such as Salomon Smith Barney's CoRTs (Corporate Backed Trust Securities), Paine Webber's CABCOs (Corporate Asset Backed Corps), and Lehman Brothers' CBTCS (Corporate Backed Trust Securities), among others (TIERs, SATURN, and so on).

While this gambit may solve the pricing inefficiency problem, you're still left with the risks of holding the underlying bonds, which are often of long maturity and low credit quality. You get the credit quality of the underlying bond, not that of the prestigious financial corporation that repackaged them. For example, some of these offerings had to be liquidated recently, after the underlying securities stopped filing the SEC paperwork required for bonds to be held in this wrapper. Since the liquidation price was less than the purchase price, this left the brokerage houses with a difficult decision: either take the hit themselves, or pass the losses on to the smaller investors who bought the repackaged bonds from them. As of this writing, it's expected that they'll decide to pass the losses on, along with their deep regrets. Meanwhile, their large institutional customers (who own the bonds in their original, un-repackaged form) will remain unaffected.

High-Grade Municipal Bonds

Ask yourself this question: Do you pay taxes? If so, you might be a good candidate for municipal bonds (or *munis*).

People buy municipal bonds to hold in taxable accounts when the after-tax yields of these bonds are higher than the equivalent yield from taxable treasury or corporate bonds. Municipal bonds are free from federal taxes, and if you buy bonds from your home state, are typically free from state (and possibly local) taxes as well. After-tax yields on municipal bonds are nearly always higher than yields available from taxable bonds of equivalent credit quality and maturity. Comparing yields from some bond mutual funds that (in spite of the different names) are closely matched for maturity and credit quality is suggestive, as you can see in Table 5.10.

Table 5.10: After-Tax Yields of Muni vs. Taxable Bond Funds 09/2004						
		After-Tax Yield by Tax Bracket				
Short-Term	**Yield**	*35%*	*33%*	*28%*	*25%*	*15%*
Vanguard Short-Term Corporate Bond	3.5%					
Vanguard Limited-Term Tax Exempt	2.9%	4.5%	4.4%	4.1%	3.9%	3.4%
Intermediate-Term						
Vanguard Int.-Term Treasury Index	4.4%					
Vanguard Int.-Term Tax Exempt	4.0%	6.2%	6.0%	5.6%	5.4%	4.7%

To facilitate making the comparison for you, we'll provide a link to a taxable-to-tax-free yield comparison tool on our Website.

Municipal bonds span the bond universe: There are municipal-bond money market funds (including single-state money market funds), municipal junk bonds—municipal bonds of every credit quality and maturity. If you run out of room to stash fixed-income investments in your tax-deferred accounts, you should certainly be taking a hard look at using municipal bonds for a portion of your taxable portfolio. But the hazardous condition of some state and local finances means you need to approach them with caution. As much as we love municipal bonds, we aren't big believers in making a total bet on them for the entirety of a bond portfolio, as some retirees do. This move exposes you to too much legislative risk (the risk that Congress might rescind their tax exemption).

Nor do we think you should bet the farm on the municipal bonds of your home state (with apologies to our own Governor Schwarzenegger). By all means, buy some local bonds if you live in a high-tax state, but diversify away from home with national munis as well. We recommend purchasing these through the intermediary of a no-load, low-expense mutual fund, where you can get pricing power and diversification. Table 5.11 lists a number of municipal bond funds that should be competitive with the taxable bond funds we've mentioned earlier in this chapter.

Table 5.11: Municipal Bond Funds 09/2004					
	Ticker	Yield	Maturity	Credit	Expense
Short Term					
Fidelity Spartan Short-Term Muni	FSTFX	2.6%	3.3 yrs	AA	0.47%
USAA Tax-Exempt Short	USSTX	2.5%	1.9 yrs	A	0.56%
Vanguard Ltd.-Term Tax Exempt	VMLTX	2.9%	2.5 yrs	AA	0.17%
Vanguard Short-Term Tax Exempt	VWSTX	1.8%	1.2 yrs	AAA	0.17%
Intermediate Term					
Fidelity Spartan Int.-Term Muni	FLTMX	3.9%	8.4 yrs	AA	0.43%
USAA Tax-Exempt Int.-Term	USATX	4.4%	8.3 yrs	AA	0.51%
Vanguard Int.-Term Tax Exempt	VWITX	4.0%	5.8 yrs	AAA	0.17%

Vanguard's offerings in this category are among the best, due to Vanguard's low expense ratios and massive purchasing power. Municipal bonds are also sold as closed-end funds, and this is as good a place as any to pause and explain the difference.

Open- vs. Closed-End Mutual Funds

An open-end mutual fund is one where management sells and redeems shares of the fund themselves at the day's closing net-asset value. Investors buy and sell their shares in the fund directly from the management company (Vanguard, Fidelity, T. Rowe Price, and so on), which in turn buys and sells the underlying securities that the fund holds (stocks, bonds, whatever) to keep pace with this supply and demand.

A closed-end fund, on the other hand, issues shares only once, at the initial public offering. After that, their shares trade like ordinary stocks on the stock exchange where they're listed. This protects the fund from massive inflows and outflows of dollars, which can confuse performance by flooding management with money or by compelling sales, and allows management to concentrate on the primary job of managing the portfolio. Since no new monies are added to the fund from new investors, the fund management company may open several near-identical closed-end funds to capture more assets, since (as with open-end funds) fees are based on total assets under management. This means that, within the closed-end fund sponsoring company (BlackRock, Nuveen, etc.), many funds tend to be run by the same managers with the same investment objectives, holding the same securities, and performing similarly.

You can read the prospectuses and scratch your head looking for a difference that really isn't there. Of course, a management company might also offer many types of funds even within a single category (muni bond, long-term bond, and so on), so you can't assume they're necessarily all the same, either.

Here's something really interesting about closed-end mutual funds: They usually trade on the open market at a premium or a discount to the actual net asset value of the securities they hold. The typical pattern is for the funds initially to be sold for more than the price of the underlying assets (to include the brokers' commissions), and then for the price to sink below the total value of these securities a few months after the initial buying frenzy passes. This pattern isn't random. The brokers who earned the commissions selling the initial public offering don't want their clients to see a dramatic initial loss on their newly purchased investments, so their firms tend to maintain buying pressure for a time to prop up the price. But then after a couple of months, they stop, and the funds often sell at a discount. Economists don't fully understand why most closed-end funds sell at a discount, but the fact is that they do. It probably has something to do with a big word in the investment world: "fear." In this case, it is "fear" of management's ability.

Closed-end funds are not to be confused with *closed funds*, which are really open-end mutual funds whose management has temporarily shut the door to new investors because they have more cash than they know what to do with.

As long as we're explaining the different types of mutual funds, we need to say a word about exchange-traded funds (ETFs). So far, we've mentioned three of these: iShares' SHY, which tracks the Lehman one- to three-year Treasury Bond Index; iShares' TIP, which tracks the Lehman Treasury Inflation Protected Security Index; and iShares' AGG, which tracks the Lehman Aggregate Bond Index. Technically, all closed-end funds are exchange-traded funds, since they're traded on stock exchanges, but ETFs usually refer to a subset of closed-end funds that are really like a hybrid of open- and closed-end funds. Instead of issuing a fixed number of shares (like closed-end funds), the management companies of these ETFs create and redeem shares to keep pace with market demand (like open-end funds). Because of this flexibility, the price of ETFs usually tracks that of the underlying securities quite closely, which means they sell at a tiny premium or discount at most.

Management expenses for these funds are also generally much lower than for funds that are actively managed. ETFs were designed to be used as building blocks, allowing investors to create portfolios with precise and stable characteristics. This winning combination of low expenses and precise asset-class targeting means that you should take a special interest in ETFs whenever they meet your needs.

You can buy most retail open-end funds directly from a mutual fund company for no commission, which is an excellent way to go if you're a long-term investor who's making regular contributions to an account. Also, you can elect to have all dividends and capital gains reinvested without charge, making it easy to capture the long-term benefits of compounding your savings.

Closed-end funds, though, trade like stocks, which means you have to pay commissions when you buy and sell them. This also means that you can buy or sell them any time the market is open, while with open-end funds you have to redeem your shares at the day's closing price. Closed-end funds normally pay out their dividends and capital gains, rather than reinvesting them, which is preferable if you're using them for current income.

While getting standardized information about open-end mutual funds on the Internet or at the library is easy (thanks to Morningstar), these closed-end funds require a lot of digging to determine their yields, the amount of leverage they employ, their expense ratios, and the tax status of their dividends. Two good places for further research are **www.etfconnect.com** and **www.cefa.com**, should you be so inclined, although you may not get the same answers at both places.

After going through all this explanation, we'd hoped to find some closed-end muni bond funds to recommend. They form the largest single category of closed-end funds, by a wide margin. However, every one we examined had risk factors that made it unsuitable for the plain-Jane bonds we deal with here: They were concentrated in one state or one market sector, held bonds of long maturities or with high levels of credit risk, they used borrowed money (called *leverage*—more on this shortly) to achieve their yields, or some combination of these practices.

These factors were enough to catapult them into our next chapter, which discusses higher-yielding bonds.

CHAPTER SIX

Higher-Yielding Bonds

The bonds we describe here have more "Tabasco" than the bonds we talked about previously. This means that they can spice up your portfolios, but they also have the power to burn. In each case, the beauty of a higher yield is paired with the beast of a greater risk—including some new hazards we haven't yet discussed. We caution you: Don't make the investments in this chapter the totality of your income portfolio.

Foreign Bonds

Marshall McLuhan pointed out that when Sputnik was launched, planet Earth became the content of its own reality TV show, and maybe something like this has happened with bond investing. A lattice of information systems now envelops the globe, and with the instantaneous flow of data across borders and around the world, new markets have developed for information-intensive regional financial offerings such as stocks and bonds from far-off lands. Ordinary investors sitting in Biloxi, Mississippi, or Racine, Wisconsin, now have the option of diversifying their holdings into foreign bonds, which might be issued by foreign governments or companies located abroad. It's a comparatively new opportunity, one that merits attention.

Let's begin with the fact that foreign investing weighs in with two entirely new risk factors: sovereign risk and currency risk.

Sovereign Risk

Sovereign risk is the danger that a country to which you lend your money might not be willing or able to repay its loans. Countries such as England and Canada have historically been good bets, while those that you can't find on a map or whose names you don't know how to spell might not be as sound.

Currency Risk

Currency risk is the possibility that the exchange rate will turn against you when the time comes to collect. For example, when you buy German bonds, your dollars are converted to euros at the prevailing rates. Then, when you collect dividends or your principal is returned, you're paid in euros. When you convert those euros back, they may be worth more or fewer dollars than before, according to the then-current exchange rates. This is the joker in the deck of foreign-bond investing.

Currency risk can, however, be hedged away. Foreign-bond traders can buy forward-exchange contracts to trade currencies at predetermined rates in the future on a schedule that matches each of the interest payments, as well as the principal repayment. If the value of the foreign currency subsequently drops in value, they make money in the process. But if they hedge unnecessarily, they forfeit the advantage that the favorable exchange rate would have given them—and paid for the privilege. Hedging currency risk costs money, and it's subtracted from the yield.

Figure 6.1 shows the average monthly risks and returns from three investment classes: intermediate-term U.S. Treasury bonds, hedged sovereign foreign bonds, and the performance of the same foreign bonds without the benefit of the currency hedging in place. Once again, the risks here refer to the fluctuation of the prices, not the default risk. The data was kindly provided to us by Merrill Lynch, and runs from 1986 to 2002; the foreign sovereignties include the United Kingdom, Europe, Canada, Australia, New Zealand, and Japan.

Figure 6.1: Foreign Bonds 1986–2002

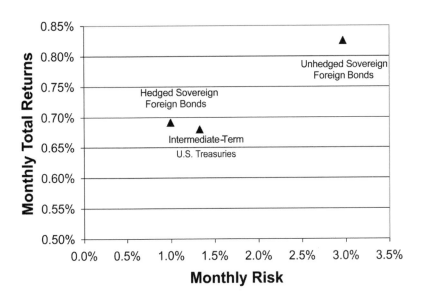

What is Figure 6.1 showing you? The hedged sovereign bonds of foreign countries had roughly the same monthly return over this 16-year period as did the U.S. Treasuries, but 0.33 percent less monthly variability. Don't get too excited, though: The index operates in a frictionless world where currency hedging is free. In the real world, currency hedging costs money, and those costs are subtracted directly from the monthly returns, so you should take the total returns of the hedged foreign bonds down a bit. While at any given time some countries offer more attractive yields than those available in the U.S., in aggregate, the global bond markets are fairly efficient.

Since the risks and returns of U.S. and hedged foreign bonds are so close, the higher returns of the unhedged bonds (in the upper right-hand corner of Figure 6.1), as well as their greater risk, stem from the addition of currency risk to the hopper.

It's interesting to note that in spite of the exposure to different markets in developed economies around the world, each with its own yield curve, *investing in unhedged foreign bonds seems largely to operate as a play on the dollar versus foreign currencies.* With the slide in the U.S. dollar lately, this foreign diversification has worked in investors' favor.

Why would conservative investors like us suggest acquiring a *riskier* asset? Portfolio managers are always eager to find investments whose performance is uncorrelated, where one zigs when the other zags. When these are combined, the variability of each component cancels out that of the other to some extent (as one is up when the other is down, and vice versa), producing an overall risk level that's lower than that of either asset taken individually. Harry Markowitz, among others, figured this out in 1951 and eventually collected a Nobel Prize for it. It is the central insight behind *modern portfolio theory.*

Consider the case of U.S. Treasury bonds and unhedged foreign-sovereign bonds, from 1986 to 1999. Let's look at the annual risk (standard deviation) and return of each asset separately, and then combined in a portfolio containing 70 percent U.S. bonds and 30 percent unhedged foreign sovereigns (see Figure 6.2).

Figure 6.2: U.S./Foreign Portfolio 1986–1999

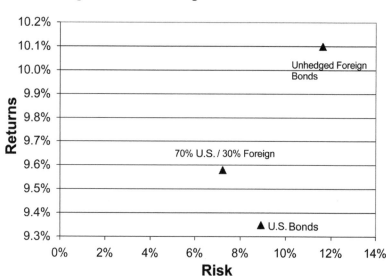

As before, the unhedged foreign bonds have higher returns and risks than the U.S. bonds alone, thanks to the vicissitudes of currency-exchange rates. But through the power of diversification, the portfolio containing 70 percent U.S. bonds and 30 percent unhedged foreign bonds adds to the annual returns while subtracting from the annual risks. We must point out, however, that this is only a 13-year sampling, and future results may differ.

Overall, hedged foreign bonds do about as well as U.S. bonds. Unhedged foreign bonds do better when the dollar is falling against the local currency, and U.S. securities succeed when the dollar is rising. Table 6.1 displays some funds that traffic in unhedged foreign bonds.

Table 6.1: Unhedged Foreign Bond Funds 09/2004					
Fund	**Ticker**	**Yield**	**Maturity**	**Credit**	**Expense**
Open-End					
T. Rowe Price Intl. Bond	RPIBX	2.4%	6.4 yrs	AA	0.91%
Black Rock Intl. Bond	CIFIX	3.7%	6.2 yrs	AAA	1.24%
Closed-End					
Aberdeen Global Income	FCO	5.6%	7.8 yrs	AA	1.91%

Unfortunately, the yields from the open-end mutual funds here aren't sufficiently high for us to recommend them to income-oriented investors.

The closed-end Aberdeen Global Income Fund, on the other hand, invests primarily in sovereign bonds from the U.K., Canada, Australia, and New Zealand—countries that aren't going anywhere soon—and offers the kind of high yield that makes it attractive to income-oriented investors. If the U.S. dollar is on a long-term decline compared to these currencies, this could be a useful hedge. On the other hand, if the dollar appreciates, this will work against you. We wish that there were other unhedged foreign bond closed-end funds, but as of today there aren't, so it's Aberdeen's way or the highway. Since we preach a gospel of diversification, we do think it could make a useful addition to the aggressive income seeker's holdings. (In addition, the decline in the dollar—somewhere between serious and stunning—shows no sign of abating, thus adding to Aberdeen's appeal.)

You may wonder: How can Aberdeen achieve this high yield when investing in high-quality intermediate-maturity bonds? The answer: Through the use of leverage.

Leverage

Leverage here refers to the practice of borrowing money at one rate with the intention of investing the proceeds at a higher rate, and then pocketing the difference. This technique is employed in a wide variety of closed-end funds. Three-quarters of all closed-end funds that invest in income securities are leveraged to some degree.

During the NASDAQ bubble, many investors found themselves making so much money so effortlessly that they went "on margin" to boost their returns. That is, the brokerage houses lent them money against the value of their stocks, charging interest against these collateralized loans. As the portfolios rocketed up 20 or 30 percent per year or more, it was chump change for investors to pay their brokers 9 or 10 percent for the loan. Leverage enabled individual investors to compound their gains on a much larger total portfolio and get rich that much faster.

Then a sad thing happened. The market imploded, and the leverage that helped propel investors into their champagne wishes and caviar dreams went into reverse, pushing them right over a cliff. Leverage, they learned, works both ways.

Maybe you think that you'd never use this dangerous-sounding investing technique. But what about your house? Taking out a mortgage loan is a classic example of using leverage. It affords you a much bigger exposure to the housing market than is possible with your down payment alone. People sometimes think that they're only in the housing market for the amount of their down payment, but this is an illusion. If your home appreciates, you realize that appreciation on its total market price. However, if it falls in value, the mortgage lender will still want the full value of its loan returned, with interest, no matter how low the price of your house sinks.

Closed-end funds use leverage by borrowing money and investing the proceeds in still more assets, jacking up the yield in the process (since it now earns interest on a bigger pot of investment money). There are various ways for them to do this (for example, by issuing preferred stock, short-term commercial paper, or getting a bank loan or a revolving-credit line), but it usually boils down to *borrowing at short maturity and lending at longer maturity, and making money on the difference in rates between the two.* This is sometimes referred to as the *carry trade.* The fund managers collect the higher yields, pay off the short-term note holders, cover their own salaries and expenses, and then distribute the remainder to shareholders.

Consider two hypothetical funds—one leveraged, the other not—in Table 6.2.

Table 6.2: Unleveraged vs. Leveraged Fund		
	Unleveraged	**Leveraged**
Starting Assets	$100.00	$100.00
Borrowed Assets	$0.00	$50.00
Total Assets	**$100.00**	**$150.00**
5% Yield Earned	$5.00	$7.50
Pay 2% on Borrowed Money	$0.00	$1.00
Total Payout	**$5.00**	**$6.50**

Both of these funds collect $100 from their investors. The ordinary, unleveraged fund invests its money in long-term bonds paying 5 percent interest, or $5. Come distribution time, management pays out these $5 to the fund's shareholders.

In the leveraged fund, management collects $100 from investors, but then sells $50 worth of short-term bonds paying 2 percent interest. This gives them a total kitty of $150 to invest in longer-term bonds paying 5 percent interest. Management collects the 5 percent interest on this $150 (or $7.50), and then it pays back the short-term bondholders 2 percent on their $50 investment—$1.00. Presto! This leaves $6.50 for distribution to fund shareholders on the same collective $100 investment. Through the magic of leverage, they obtain 6.5 percentage points of yield instead of 5—a 30 percent improvement. Archimedes (who said that with the proper leverage he could move the earth) would have been proud.

Although this may seem to be a free-money machine, it isn't. The investors in the leveraged fund have assumed a higher degree of risk. Their fund can be expected to display far more price volatility, since they're exposed to $150 worth of market risk for their $100 investment (just as you're exposed to the total market-price change of your home, even if you only made a 20 percent down payment). If interest rates rise, the fund value will fall faster, too.

In 1994, the Federal Reserve raised short-term interest rates by 2 percent, ultimately causing leveraged-bond funds to fall 20 percent in value. Between 1999 and 2001, the Federal Reserve raised short-term rates 1.75 percentage points. This caused leveraged municipal-bond funds to fall 12 percent on average, and lower-credit-quality bond funds fell 28 percent due to increased defaults. In April 2004, a whisper of higher interest rates created carnage on a huge scale in leveraged fixed income of all kinds. On the other hand, if interest rates fall, the funds' value will rise much faster than those that are unleveraged.

In addition to the *direction* interest rates might go (up versus down), there's risk from the *spread* in interest rates (high versus low). The steeper the rising yield curve, relating again to yields and maturities, the more money there is to be made through leverage. While most of the time, long-term rates are higher than short-term rates, this isn't always the case. Occasionally, the yield curve is inverted, and short-term rates go higher than long-term rates. Even if it's relatively flat, "borrowing short and lending long" can be a losing proposition after expenses. If both short- and long-term interest rates rise in tandem, some of the benefits of leverage can endure, as long as the spread between them remains constant.

Depending on the type of security the fund invests in, a "ceiling" will be in place—a point past which leverage no longer is profitable. For a real-estate fund, this would be the yield from the rents it collects, while for a stock-dividend fund, this would be the yield from its stock portfolio. For a bond fund, this would be the yield from its underlying bonds. If short-term borrowing costs rise above the yield from these rents or dividends or coupons, leverage fails to add value. Eventually, the yields on all these types of underlying securities might increase (rents, dividends, coupons), but short-term rates can increase faster, squeezing a fund into an unprofitable condition.

Nonetheless, for the aggressive fixed-income investor, *there's no inherent reason why the greater monthly price volatility of the leveraged fund should be a problem, as long as the higher yield remains constant.* In a world of necessary trade-offs and compromises, it's perfectly rational for income investors to accept wider swings in the market price of their assets as the price for achieving a sustained higher yield.

Be reassured that under most circumstances, leverage increases yield. Near the end of 2004, for example, a sampling of leveraged municipal bond funds offered an additional 1.2 percentage points of yield over those that were unleveraged.

What's more, used judiciously, these funds may provide a measure of time diversification. In a high-interest-rate environment, numerous sources of high returns are available to income investors. In a low-interest-rate world, however, the added leverage can make a difference to your quality of life, and an asset that pays you more when you need it the most is nothing to ignore.

Theoretically, you could leverage your own investment accounts and achieve the same result by going on margin. But as a small individual investor, you won't be able to borrow money at anything like the low interest rates available to the giant investment companies who are borrowing millions. For the municipal-bond investor, there's another problem: Borrowing via a margin account to buy tax-free securities is illegal. Closed-end municipal-bond funds, however, can do so.

Income investors tend to be conservative and hate to take risks with their principal. The last thing you want to do is to sell in panic when the value of your accounts has fallen. Many of these leveraged funds are new, so it's difficult to predict exactly how they'll behave. It might be instructive to consider the fates of two similar funds (one leveraged, the other not), which have been around for the past decade. The leveraged fund is Nuveen Municipal Market Opportunity (NMO), and the unleveraged fund is Nuveen Municipal Value (NUV). They hold a nationally diversified, long-term (approximately 21 years average maturity) portfolio of municipal bonds of similar credit quality (AA-rated portfolios, on average). Figure 6.3 shows their market prices from 1990 to 2003.

Figure 6.3: Price—Leveraged vs. Unleveraged Bond Funds

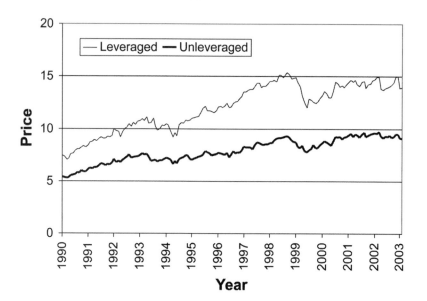

The period under study has been favorable for bond investing, redounding to the benefit of the leveraged fund. While it's up more overall, the ride has been rockier. Look at the period from 1999 to 2000: Not only was this a time when the NASDAQ was going through the roof and making investors wonder why they were holding bonds at all, but leveraged funds fell much more during this time than did unleveraged funds (from peak to trough). In 1999, you'd have felt doubly like a chump for owning a leveraged-bond fund. These are the times that try investors' souls.

But, in hindsight, would you really have been a chump? After all, a few years later, the NASDAQ was down 75 percent, while your leveraged bond fund was up 12 percent. Meanwhile, your monthly dividend payout would have been consistently higher than if you'd gone the unleveraged route. During the worst period (March 1999 to April 2000), your yield still would have been 7.32 percent in the leveraged fund versus 6.07 percent if unleveraged.

As Figure 6.4 shows, the total returns from owning the leveraged fund were better over the entire period.

Figure 6.4: Total Returns of Leveraged vs. Unleveraged Funds

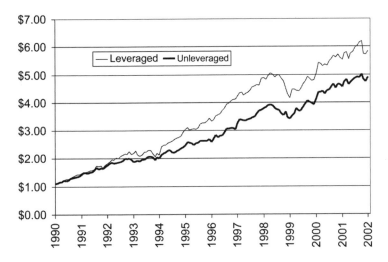

Income investors, however, are primarily interested in the income stream an investment generates. Figure 6.5 tellingly shows the results of having invested $100 in each of these funds at the beginning of 1991, tracking the sum of the checks that arrived in the mail every month: dividends and distributed capital gains.

Figure 6.5: Income from Leveraged vs. Unleveraged Funds

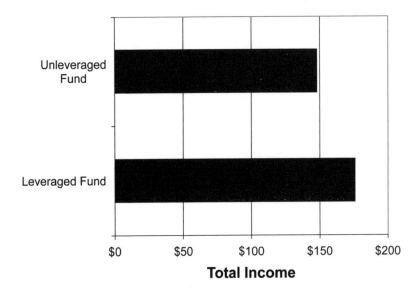

Total Income

Although income investors rode out more ups and downs along the way in terms of the value of their portfolio, they pocketed 19 percent more cash over this period by leveraging their initial investment. Had they started with $100,000 instead of $100, they would have received an extra $28,171 in spending money over the 13-year period, most of it tax-free. But before you break out the party hats, remember that in the awful April of 2004, the unleveraged NUV was down 6.9 percent, and the leveraged NMO was down 11.9 percent. These price fluctuations are real, and they can be painful.

In consideration of these factors, risk-tolerant income investors might want to consider using leveraged funds for a portion of their portfolios. The basic principles we've discussed here apply to the other types of leveraged closed-end funds that we'll discuss later, including municipal-bond funds, leveraged preferred and dividend stock funds, and leveraged real estate investment trust funds.

Emerging Market Bonds

Lending your money to Canada or England is one thing. What about lending it to the likes of Uruguay, Bulgaria, or the Ivory Coast? Should you lend to countries where you wouldn't drink the water?

Check out the yields and three-year annualized returns from the hottest emerging-market-debt mutual funds (many of these only available to institutional investors) in Table 6.3.

Table 6.3: Emerging Market Bond Funds 09/2004		
Fund	Yield	3-Yr Return
GMO Emerging Country Debt	10.5%	25.0%
Salomon Brothers Instl. Emg. Market Debt	7.5%	19.4%
Federated International High Income A	9.3%	18.5%
AllianceBernstein Emg. Market Debt	7.6%	23.7%

A 10 percent yield? Who wouldn't want that? A 25 percent annualized total return, over a period when stocks defenestrated themselves? Walk away from that temptation, if you can.

To put this in perspective, consider Figure 6.6, which shows unhedged emerging market bond returns and risks (the monthly standard deviation of returns) since 1991 (courtesy of Merrill Lynch), again compared with intermediate-term U.S. Treasuries and the unhedged sovereign foreign bonds from their developed market brothers.

Figure 6.6: Monthly Risk & Returns of Emerging Market Debt 1992–2003

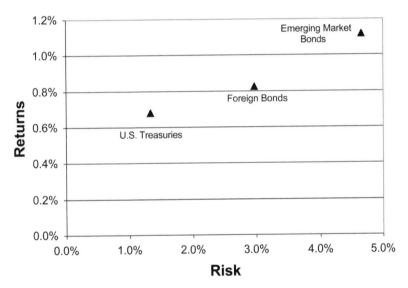

As you might expect, lending money to emerging market countries has a colorful history. Often, these economies are driven by demand for natural resources. When the price of oil dropped during the 1980s, for example, Mexico defaulted on its loan payments to U.S. banks, creating a crisis of staggering proportions. Commercial banks had lent billions of dollars to Latin America, and now all those loans were in jeopardy.

The United States, in conjunction with the International Monetary Fund, found a way to let Mexico (and then other countries) restructure their debt, offering a mixture of debt forgiveness and lower interest rates on the balances. The plan was named after former Secretary of the Treasury Nicholas Brady. To make sure that the debt would continue to be liquid, the United States agreed to underwrite the loans' principal, backing it with zero-coupon Treasury bonds.

In effect, these "Brady bonds" promoted the emerging debt into dollar-denominated securities. Even if Mexico defaulted on making the coupon payments, the U.S. Treasury promised to pay back the principal when the bonds matured. (Try getting a deal like that from your local bank next time you miss a mortgage payment!) The emerging market debt had simply become too big to fail. Pretty soon, the United States had issued $170 billion worth of these securities.

Incredibly, this means that you can buy high-yielding, dollar-denominated bonds from countries such as Vietnam, Nigeria, and Jordan whose principal is backed by . . . U.S. Treasuries. Not all emerging market debt consists of Brady bonds, but a sizable percentage of it does (exact amounts vary by country). Unfortunately for income investors, many of them had call provisions and are being recalled to refund the debt at new, lower rates.

People buy these bonds not for their guaranteed return of principal, but for the sweet yields they promise, although the ride has been anything but smooth. Investors got an unpleasant jolt in 1998 when Russia defaulted on its Soviet-era debt (while maintaining payments on its post-Soviet debt). Some emerging market bond funds dropped 34 percent that year, and that's exactly the kind of roller-coaster ride you have to expect.

Because the securities are difficult to value and subject to a variety of risks, aggressive income investors will want to include a small amount of emerging market debt in their fixed-income portfolios. Some funds to consider are listed in Table 6.4.

Note that the closed-end funds here all employ leverage to enhance their yields. This adds the risk of leverage to the uncertainty of emerging markets—a cocktail that may be too heady for some.

Table 6.4: Emerging Market Bond Funds 09/2004			
Fund	**Ticker**	**Yield**	**Expense**
OPEN-END FUNDS			
Fidelity New Market Income	FNMIX	5.7%	1.00%
T. Rowe Price Emerging Markets Bond	PREMX	6.0%	1.10%
CLOSED-END FUNDS			
Global High Income Dollar Fund	GHI	10.9%	1.42%
Morgan Stanley Emg. Markets Debt	MSD	8.0%	1.25%
Salomon Emg. Markets Income II	EDF	7.4%	1.98%
Salomon Emg. Markets Income Float.	EFL	7.6%	2.36%
Scudder Global High Income	LBF	7.4%	2.28%
Templeton Emerging Markets Income	TEI	7.6%	1.17%

Leveraged Municipal-Bond Funds

By far, the biggest category of leveraged closed-end funds is national and single-state municipal-bond funds. Unfortunately, we can't recommend most of them. Not because they're leveraged, but because of the types of bonds they contain. We've already expressed our reservations about long-term bonds, which give too little yield for their added interest-rate risk. This problem is magnified in the present low-rate environment, where interest rates have little room to fall (increasing the value of existing bonds) but plenty of room to rise (decreasing existing-bond prices). Leveraging these risks makes this investment unacceptable, in our view.

The other problem is that many of these funds hold municipal junk bonds. We aren't fans of junk bonds, and municipal ones are among the most toxic. If we didn't like junk in the first place, we'd like leveraging it even less, so we've omitted these funds as well.

Table 6.5 contains a short list of some leveraged municipal-bond funds to consider. These have been screened for lower expense ratios, higher credit quality and shorter maturities than most, and include a few single-state municipal-bond funds.

Table 6.5: Leveraged Municipal Bond Closed-End Funds 09/2004

Fund	Ticker	Yield	Maturity	Credit	Expense
NATIONAL					
BlackRock Ins. Muni Term Trust 2010	BMT	5.7%	6.8 yrs	AAA	1.02%
BlackRock Ins. Muni Term Trust 2008	BRM	5.9%	5.6 yrs	AAA	0.98%
Federated Premium Intermediate	FPT	5.4%	8.1 yrs	A	0.80%
Eaton Vance Insured Muni	EIM	6.4%	12.6 yrs	AAA	0.73%
Eaton Vance Insured Muni 2	EIV	6.6%	11.1 yrs	AAA	0.84%
SINGLE STATE					
Eaton Vance Michigan	MIW	6.4%	9.9 yrs	AAA	1.09%
Eaton Vance New York	ENX	5.8%	9.4 yrs	AAA	0.79%
Eaton Vance Pennsylvania	EIP	6.5%	8.5 yrs	AAA	0.97%
Eaton Vance California	EVM	6.4%	9.8 yrs	AAA	0.77%
Eaton Vance New Jersey	EMJ	6.3%	11.8 yrs	AAA	0.99%
Eaton Vance Ohio	EIO	6.4%	10.2 yrs	AAA	0.99%

A word is in order about the BlackRock Term Trust funds. A common objection to holding bonds in a mutual-fund format is that the bond fund never matures, so there's no promised return of principal at the end of the rainbow. The managers are perpetually buying and selling bonds, redeeming one to buy another. If you hold an individual bond, you always have the option of clinging to it until it matures, at which point you get back its face value. Even if interest rates have risen since you bought it and the bond now sells at a substantial discount, on the day it matures, you get all your money back (if the bond hasn't defaulted).

BlackRock has neatly sidestepped this problem by offering several bond funds containing securities that all mature on a given year. The BlackRock Advisors Insured Muni Term Trust 2008 (ticker: BRM) is going to put itself out of business in 2008, when the bonds that it holds are redeemed and the proceeds mailed back to shareholders. This gives you the advantages of leverage and diversification, and of using the expertise and mass purchasing power of a major investment company to select and buy bonds on your behalf, along with the comparative certainty of getting your principal returned to you in 2008 (or 2010 for BlackRock's BMT), no matter how interest rates rise or fall in the meantime.

This brings our discussion of bonds temporarily to an end. Now we'll move on and examine what role stocks should play for the income investor.

CHAPTER SEVEN

Stocks for Income

In olden days, stocks used to pay big dividends: In the 1930s and 1940s, the average dividend yield on the S&P 500 levitated between 4 and 8 percent. This was especially remarkable in the 1930s, when the price level was rapidly dropping for a good part of the decade, which meant that the real yield on dividend-paying stocks was astronomical. Even during the great decade of the 1950s, the yield on the Dow stocks often exceeded the yield on high-grade corporate bonds. During the 1970s and '80s, it ranged between 3 and 5 percent, dropping below 2 percent in the '90s. As of this writing in October of 2004, the dividend yield on the S&P 500 stands at a pitiful 1.8 percent. The yield on the Dow Jones Industrial Average is higher, but still only about 2.1 percent.

Figure 7.1 shows the dividend yield since 1918. Note the direction of the trend line: down.

Figure 7.1: S&P 500 Dividend Yield 1918–2003

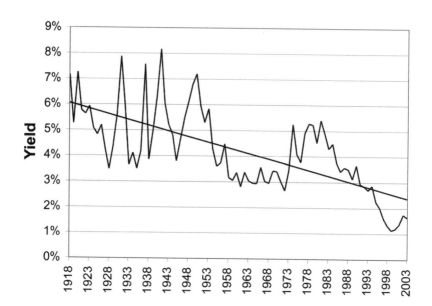

Recall that, historically, the dividends that stocks paid accounted for 70 percent of the real gains from stock market investing. This yield has shrunk dramatically. Why did this happen? There are several reasons.

First, dividends are "double-taxed." That is, they're taxed once as income at the corporate level, and then they're taxed again as ordinary income when they're distributed to shareholders. So it made a certain amount of sense for corporations to retain their earnings and put them to work elsewhere: paying down debt, investing in new capital equipment, purchasing or starting new businesses, or even buying back their own stock on the open market. This way, shareholders would theoretically get the benefit of a capital appreciation in the stock price.

Since capital gains, when realized, were taxed at a lower rate than dividends, this arrangement worked to investors' advantage— or so the thinking went. But these retained earnings had a double effect: making stocks more volatile while simultaneously reducing dividends. Income-oriented investors desired neither.

Of course, embedded in this philosophy was a certain amount of hubris on the part of management. Corporate CEOs invariably felt that their sixth-best idea for using company profits was better than their shareholders' best investment ideas. This conceit turns out to be wrong. Robert Arnott, editor of *Financial Analysts Journal*, and Clifford Asness, president and managing principal of AQR Capital Management, have examined the record and found that high dividends typically foreshadowed *higher* corporate earnings in subsequent years, not the other way around. A lot of empire building occurs at shareholders' expense, not for shareholders' benefit. Some cynics have even speculated that the real reason for retaining dividends has been nothing more than management's desire to have more money to play with in their gilded sandboxes.

Another factor leading to the falling dividend yield in the 1990s was the tech boom. Growth stocks notoriously burn through their earnings—if any—to expand their enterprises. As the compilers of the S&P 500 Index loaded up on high-tech growth stocks during the bubble to increase the index's "sex appeal," this crowded out the traditional dividend-paying companies. Dividend investors felt like old fogeys during the tech bubble, as their bricks-and-mortar stocks were completely disdained by tech investors, and the tech stocks reached staggering heights—at least until the bubble burst.

However, there are still some stocks that pay a good dividend. Thanks to President Bush, the Jobs and Growth Tax Relief Reconciliation Act of 2003 has lowered the top tax rate on dividends from 39 percent to 15 percent (and it's down to only 5 percent for taxpayers in the lowest tax brackets). *The dividend investor in the top bracket now gets to keep 39 percent more money than he did before.*

There's an important exception: Taxpayers stuck in the quagmire of the Alternative Minimum Tax find themselves taxed at roughly 28 percent of their dividends, no matter what the rest of the tax code says. Even so, now that the tax argument for withholding dividends is greatly weakened (since dividends are now taxed at the same rate as capital gains), we're hopeful that companies will start ponying up dividends once again. You'd expect the market for high-dividend-paying stocks to have shot up under the circumstances, but so far, it hasn't (although we think it will, eventually). In the meantime, the newspapers are full of stories of companies raising their paltry dividends to accommodate the new tax landscape—even Microsoft pays a dividend now.

Certain sectors of the stock market have historically rewarded investors with high dividend yields. Often, these are industries that were tightly regulated, like public utilities or banks. Sometimes they're companies with limited prospects for growth, such as those selling natural resources like timber or chemicals. They can also be mature companies that experience a steady demand for their products, like food and medical supplies. If a recession hits, people might put off that trip to the Seychelles or buying a new Mercedes S-Class sedan, but they aren't going to stop drinking Pepsi or using electricity. They'll continue to heat their houses, buy underwear, and chew gum. Noncyclical companies that make inexpensive, nondurable consumer goods usually have a steady flow of income available to divert to shareholders, and these companies are about to become your new best friends. (Still another market sector that pays handsome dividends is commercial real estate, which we're saving for a chapter all its own.)

The investment firm of T. Rowe Price looked at what happened (income-wise) to an investor who put $10,000 in the S&P 500 on March 31, 1984, and held it for 20 years. They compared this person's plight with someone who put $10,000 in the Lehman Brothers U.S. Aggregate Bond Index on the same date and held it for the same length of time. This is a fair trial, since both indexes represent the benchmark investments for their respective markets. So who got more cash in the mail?

Answer: The bond investor did, naturally. This individual clipped $17,776 in coupons over the 20 years. But surprisingly, the stock investor pocketed $16,372 in dividends during this same period. The person who chose stocks stayed in the running, especially when you consider that while the bond investor's portfolio grew to be worth $11,979 at the end of this period (net of coupons), the S&P 500 investor's portfolio grew to $70,750 (net of dividends). The dividends the stock investor raked in during the final year gave a yield of nearly 11 percent on the initial investment, and this during one of the most dismal dividend years in the S&P 500's history. Dividends kept rising as the stock prices went up, so even though they ended at a low percentage of stock prices in 2004, they were still high relative to the stocks' original price.

The moral: It makes sense for income-oriented investors to own dividend-paying stocks for a significant portion of their investment portfolios.

Diving for Dividends

Where should the income-oriented investor go fishing? We first looked to the mutual-fund industry, which offers more types of open-ended funds than Starbucks does coffee-flavored drinks. A list of the leading contenders appears in Table 7.1.

Table 7.1: Dividend-Oriented Mutual Funds 09/2004			
Fund	**Ticker**	**Yield**	**Expense**
Vanguard Wellesley Income Fund	VWINX	4.1%	0.31%
Berwyn Income Fund	BERIX	4.9%	0.71%
Huntington Equity Income Fund	HIEFX	1.8%	1.17%
Schwab Dividend Equity Investor	SWDIX	2.2%	1.10%

Unfortunately, this little list has big problems. The Vanguard Wellesley Income Fund has been around for years, so it was our first stop. However, 60 percent of the income in this fund comes from bonds, not stocks, meaning that it's not really a stock dividend fund. Its dividends are taxed at a hybrid rate—partly as ordinary income (the bond coupons), and partly as stock dividends. Finally, because it's an actively managed fund, the allocation between stocks and bonds could change, making it difficult to hold in a portfolio with predictable results.

The Berwyn Income Fund has the same problems as the Wellesley fund, only more so. For starters, it has nearly twice the annual expense ratio. It offers a higher yield, but 68 percent of the fund comes from bonds, and these are of lower quality than the ones the Wellesley fund holds. It also has the same hybrid tax status and the same problems fitting in with the rest of our recommendations for your portfolio.

The Huntington Equity Income Fund is a pure stock-dividend fund, but its expense ratio (1.17 percent) is too high, and its dividend yield is too low (1.8 percent). Additionally, it holds the occasional real estate investment trust, making it subject to hybrid taxation and the same problems the other actively managed funds have with allocating it in a portfolio.

The Schwab fund, the newest of the bunch, is at least a pure play on dividend stocks taxable at the top 15 percent rate: It holds no bonds or real estate investment trusts. But the expense ratio is too high for our liking. Schwab is deferring some of the expenses and capping the ratio at 1.1 percent through February of 2005, but the fund's actual expense ratio is 1.28 percent.

A new entry that merits close watching is the Alpine Dynamic Dividend Fund (ticker: ADVDX). Alpine fishes for dividends just before they're paid, and then holds the stocks for 61 days before selling. The fund has an astonishingly high yield (6.9 percent as of November 2004), but also has high fees (2.06 percent, with 0.71 percent deferred and a 1 percent short-term redemption fee). How much will the higher dividend be offset by higher short-term capital gains taxes from Alpine's short-swing trading? Stay tuned . . .

We had better luck with the closed-end fund universe. These funds are shown in table 7.2, and they bear discussing in detail.

Table 7.2: Closed-End Dividend Funds 09/2004			
Fund	Ticker	Current Yield	Expense
iShares Dow Jones Select Div. Index	DVY	3.3%	0.40%
BlackRock Div. Achievers Trust	BDV	6.0%*	0.84%
BlackRock Strategic Div. Achievers Trust	BDT	6.3%*	0.84%

* Distribution dividend may include a return of principal.

The Dow Jones Select Dividend Index

Barclays wanted to open a low-expense iShares exchange-traded fund (ETF) for dividend investors, so they hired Dow Jones to create the Select Dividend Index. The idea is that the fund will track the index, creating a one-stop solution for dividend-hungry investors.

In devising their selection, Dow Jones has done a number of things right. Their process begins with a list of the top dividend-paying stocks from the Dow Jones Total Stock Market Index. Then they narrow the list. They exclude real estate investment trusts so that all dividends are taxable at the 15 percent rate. They make sure that each of the stocks has a positive five-year dividend-growth rate, so companies whose stock prices are plummeting (creating an artificially high temporary dividend yield) aren't included. Weak players on the list are quickly replaced if their dividend yields fall and someone else's becomes more attractive, so the 50 companies making the final cut are Darwinian survivors. The companies in the Dow Jones Select Dividend Index as of this writing are shown in Table 7.3.

Table 7.3: Dow Jones Select Dividend Stocks 09/2004			
Name	Ticker	Yield	Industry
Altria Group Inc.	MO	6.2%	Tobacco
AmSouth Bancorp	ASO	3.9%	Banks
Associated Banc-Corp.	ASBC	3.1%	Banks
Bank of America Corp.	BAC	4.2%	Banks
BellSouth Corp.	BLS	4.0%	Telecommunications
Black Hills Corp.	BKH	4.5%	Utilities
Bristol-Myers Squibb Co.	BMY	4.7%	Healthcare
Citizens Banking Corp.	CBCF	3.5%	Banks
Colonial Bancgroup Inc.	CNB	2.8%	Banks
Comerica Inc.	CMA	3.5%	Banks
Dow Chemical Co.	DOW	3.0%	Chemicals
DTE Energy Co.	DTE	4.9%	Utilities
Duquesne Light Holdings Inc.	DQE	5.6%	Utilities
Eastman Chemical Co.	EMN	3.7%	Chemicals
Energy East Corp.	EAS	4.1%	Utilities
F.N.B. Corp.	FNB	4.2%	Banks
FirstEnergy Corp.	FE	3.7%	Utilities
FirstMerit Corp.	FMER	4.1%	Banks
FPL Group Inc.	FPL	4.0%	Utilities
General Motors Corp.	GM	4.7%	Automobiles
Genuine Parts Co.	GPC	3.1%	Automobiles
Hibernia Corp.	HIB	3.0%	Banks
Hudson United Bancorp	HU	3.8%	Banks
Huntington Bancshares Inc.	HBAN	3.2%	Banks
JPMorgan Chase & Co.	JPM	3.4%	Banks

Table 7.3: Dow Jones Select Dividend Stocks (cont'd.)			
Name	Ticker	Yield	Industry
KeyCorp	KEY	3.9%	Banks
Lincoln National Corp.	LNC	3.0%	Insurance
Lubrizol Corp.	LZ	3.0%	Chemicals
Lyondell Chemical Co.	LYO	4.0%	Chemicals
Marathon Oil Corp.	MRO	2.4%	Energy
MeadWestvaco Corp.	MWV	2.9%	Basic Resources
National City Corp.	NCC	3.6%	Banks
Nicor Inc.	GAS	5.1%	Utilities
NiSource Inc.	NI	4.4%	Utilities
Occidental Petroleum Corp.	OXY	2.0%	Energy
People's Bank (Bridgeport)	PBCT	3.3%	Banks
Pinnacle West Capital Corp.	PNW	4.3%	Utilities
PNC Financial Services Group	PNC	3.7%	Banks
PPG Industries Inc.	PPG	2.9%	Chemicals
PPL Corp.	PPL	3.5%	Utilities
Provident Bankshares Corp.	PBKS	3.0%	Banks
R.R. Donnelley & Sons Co.	RRD	3.3%	Industrial
RPM International Inc.	RPM	3.2%	Chemicals
SBC Communications Inc.	SBC	4.8%	Telecommunications
Sky Financial Group Inc.	SKYF	3.4%	Banks
Sonoco Products Co.	SON	3.3%	Industrial
Unitrin Inc.	UTR	4.0%	Insurance
Universal Corp.	UVV	3.5%	Tobacco
Washington Federal Inc.	WFSL	3.3%	Banks
Whitney Holding Corp.	WTNY	3.1%	Banks

If you'd put $100 into the dividend index in 1992 (a neat trick since it hadn't been created yet, but assuming that you could have), it would have been worth $315 by mid-2003, surpassing even the $279 that the same money would have been worth had it been invested in the Dow Jones Industrial Average (DJIA) over that same period. You'd have missed the entire Internet/telecom bubble and been better off for it.

Figure 7.2 is useful to consider, since it shows how dividend stocks march to a different drummer than the stock market as a whole. This chart assumes that both the Dow Jones Select Dividend Index and the Dow Jones Industrial Average had a value of 100 in 1992, and then tracks the total returns of both indexes (the value of the stocks plus the reinvested dividends and capital gains). If we stopped the competition at the end of 2000 (during the bubble), the DJIA comes out ahead. But since then, the DJIA has retrenched, while the dividend index, like the Energizer bunny, has kept on going. Owning a portfolio of dividend stocks doesn't mean that you'll be reproducing the performance of the stock market as a whole.

**Figure 7.2: Total Return on Dow Jones Dividend
vs.
Dow Jones Industrials 1992–2003**

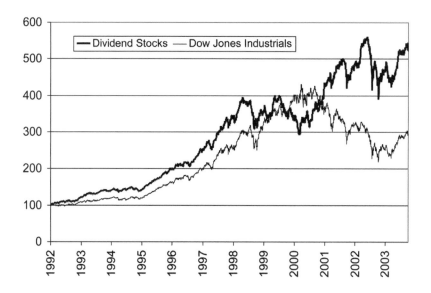

Pay special attention to the period from mid-1999 to mid-2000 on this chart. Your dividend stocks would have been sinking while the Dow Jones Industrial Average (and everything else) was soaring. You would have been the laughingstock of the cocktail party with your pathetic ideas about dividends and the old economy—the investment equivalent of ordering white zinfandel. But during the bear market beginning in 2001, non-dividend-paying stocks lost more than 5 percent, while those that paid dividends stayed level. Those that paid *significant* dividends (as shown above) took off, but dividend investors failed to gain any popularity points, as their neighbors now hated them for having been being right all along.

If you had $181,875 as of this writing, you could buy 100 shares of each of the stocks in the index and earn a similar yield (the trailing 12-month yield is unknown since this fund is relatively new, but the current yield is 3.25 percent) without having to forfeit the 0.40 percent in annual fund-management fees. The fund updates its holdings monthly, adding and dropping stocks as they meet or fail to meet the criteria for inclusion, so if you were willing to join in the hunt, you could replicate the list fairly closely. Then again, for investors with less to spend on dividend stocks, or who don't want to manage a large stock portfolio themselves, iShares DVY is a compelling drive-through solution.

But Dow Jones isn't the only one to assemble a list of dividend stocks. . . .

The Mergent Dividend Achievers

Mergent takes a different approach. While Dow Jones seeks the *highest* dividends in the stock universe, Mergent looks for those companies that have a ten-year consecutive history of *raising* their dividends. The only other consideration is liquidity—they want to make sure that these companies' stocks trade in sufficient volume that institutions can acquire and redeem shares in quantity without having their buying and selling unduly impact the price.

Table 7.4 shows a list of the Mergent Dividend Achievers. The index is reconstituted annually, and in 2004 there were 303 stocks that met Mergent's criteria.

Table 7.4 Mergent Dividend Achievers 2004

1st Source Corp.	Artesian Resources Corp.	Briggs & Stratton Corp.
3M Co.	Associated Banc-Corp.	Brown & Brown, Inc.
Abbott Laboratories	Atmos Energy Corp.	Brown-Forman Corp.
ABM Industries, Inc.	Automatic Data Processing Inc.	California Water Service Group
AFLAC Inc.	Avery Dennison Corp.	Camden Property Trust
Air Products & Chemicals, Inc.	Avon Products, Inc.	Carlisle Companies Inc.
Alberto-Culver Co.	Badger Meter, Inc.	Caterpillar Inc.
Alfa Corp.	BancFirst Corp.	Cedar Fair, L.P.
ALLTEL Corp.	BancorpSouth Inc.	CenturyTel, Inc.
Altria Group Inc.	Bandag, Inc.	Charter One Financial, Inc.
Ambac Financial Group, Inc.	Bank of America Corp.	Chemical Financial Corp.
American International Group Inc.	Bank of Hawaii Corp	ChevronTexaco Corp.
American States Water Co.	Banta Corporation	Chittenden Corp.
AmSouth Bancorporation	Bard (C.R.), Inc.	Chubb Corp.
Anchor BanCorp Wisconsin, Inc.	BB&T Corp.	Cincinnati Financial Corp.
Anheuser-Busch Cos., Inc.	Beckman Coulter, Inc.	Cintas Corporation
Applebee's International, Inc.	Becton, Dickinson and Co.	Citigroup Inc.
AptarGroup Inc.	Bemis, Inc.	Citizens Banking Corp.
Aqua America Inc.	Black Hills Corporation	Clarcor Inc.
Archer Daniels Midland Co.	Bowl America Inc.	Cleco Corp.
Arrow International,Inc.	Brady Corp.	Clorox Co.

Table 7.4 Mergent Dividend Achievers 2004 (cont'd.)

Coca-Cola Co	Dover Corp.	First Indiana Corp.
Colgate-Palmolive Co.	EastGroup Properties, Inc.	First Merchants Corp.
Comerica, Inc.	Eaton Vance Corp.	First Midwest Bancorp, Inc.
Commerce Bancorp, Inc.	Ecolab, Inc.	FirstMerit Corp
Commerce Bancshares, Inc.	Emerson Electric Co.	Florida Public Utilities Co.
Commercial Net Lease Realty, Inc.	Energen Corp.	Franklin Electric Co., Inc.
Community Bank System, Inc.	EnergySouth, Inc.	Franklin Resources, Inc.
Community First Bankshares, Inc.	Exxon Mobil Corp.	Freddie Mac
Community Trust Bancorp, Inc.	F.N.B. Corp	Frisch's Restaurants, Inc.
Compass Bancshares Inc.	Family Dollar Stores, Inc.	Fuller (H.B.) Company
ConAgra Foods, Inc.	Fannie Mae	Fulton Financial Corp.
Connecticut Water Service, Inc.	Farmer Bros. Co.	Gallagher (Arthur J.) & Co.
Consolidated Edison, Inc.	Federal Realty Investment Trust	Gannett Co., Inc.
Corus Bankshares, Inc.	Federal Signal Corp.	General Dynamics Corp.
Courier Corp.	Fidelity National Financial, Inc.	General Electric Co.
Cullen/Frost Bankers, Inc.	Fifth Third Bancorp	General Growth Properties, Inc.
CVB Financial Corp.	First Charter Corp.	Genuine Parts Co.
Danaher Corp.	First Commonwealth Financial Corp.	Glacier Bancorp, Inc.
Diebold, Inc.	First Federal Capital Corp.	Golden West Financial Corp.
Donnelley (R.R.) & Sons Co.	First Financial Corp.	Gorman-Rupp Co.
Doral Financial Corp.	First Financial Holdings, Inc.	Grainger (W.W.) Inc.

Table 7.4 Mergent Dividend Achievers 2004 (cont'd.)

Harley-Davidson, Inc.	Jefferson-Pilot Corp.	McCormick & Co., Inc.
Harleysville Group, Inc.	Johnson & Johnson	McDonald's Corp.
Harleysville National Corp.	Johnson Controls Inc.	McGrath RentCorp
Haverty Furniture Cos., Inc.	KeyCorp	McGraw-Hill Cos., Inc.
Health Care Property Investors, Inc.	Kimberly-Clark Corp.	MDU Resources Group Inc.
Healthcare Realty Trust, Inc.	Kimco Realty Corp.	Medtronic, Inc.
Heinz (H.J.) Co.	Lancaster Colony Corp.	Mercantile Bankshares Corp.
Helmerich & Payne, Inc.	La-Z-Boy Inc.	Merck & Co., Inc.
Hershey Foods Corp.	Legg Mason, Inc.	Mercury General Corp.
Hibernia Corp.	Leggett & Platt, Inc.	Meredith Corp.
Hilb, Rogal and Hamilton Co.	Lilly (Eli) & Co.	Meridian Bioscience Inc.
Hillenbrand Industries, Inc.	Lincoln National Corp.	MGE Energy Inc.
Holly Corp.	Linear Technology Corp.	Middlesex Water Co.
Home Depot, Inc.	Lowe's Cos., Inc.	Midland Co.
HON Industries Inc.	M & T Bank Corp.	Mine Safety Appliances Co.
Hormel Foods Corp.	Marsh & McLennan Cos., Inc.	Myers Industries Inc.
Hudson United Bancorp	Marshall & Ilsley Corp.	NACCO Industries Inc.
Illinois Tool Works, Inc.	Masco Corp.	National City Corp.
Independent Bank Corp.	May Department Stores Co.	National Commerce Financial Corp.
Irwin Financial Corp.	MBIA Inc.	National Fuel Gas Co.
Jack Henry & Associates, Inc.	MBNA Corp.	National Penn Bancshares, Inc.

Table 7.4 Mergent Dividend Achievers 2004 (cont'd.)

National Security Group, Inc.	Pinnacle West Capital Corp.	Sara Lee Corp.
NICOR Inc.	Pitney Bowes, Inc.	SBC Communications, Inc.
Nordson Corp.	Popular Inc.	Second Bancorp, Inc.
Northern Trust Corp.	PPG Industries, Inc.	SEI Investments Co.
Nucor Corp.	Praxair, Inc.	ServiceMaster Co.
Nuveen Investments Inc.	Procter & Gamble Co.	Sherwin-Williams Co.
Old National Bancorp	Progress Energy, Inc.	Sigma-Aldrich Corp.
Old Republic International Corp.	Progressive Corp.	Simmons First National Corp.
Otter Tail Corp.	Protective Life Corp.	SJW Corp.
Pacific Capital Bancorp	Quaker Chemical Corp.	SLM Corp.
Park National Corp.	Questar Corp.	Smith (A.O.) Corp.
Parker-Hannifin Corp.	Quixote Corp.	Sonoco Products Co.
Paychex Inc.	Raven Industries, Inc.	SouthTrust Corp.
Pennichuck Corp.	Regions Financial Corp.	St. Paul Companies, Inc.
Pentair, Inc.	Republic Bancorp, Inc.	Stanley Works
People's Bank	RLI Corp.	State Auto Financial Corp.
Peoples Energy Corp.	Rohm & Haas Co.	State Street Corp.
PepsiCo Inc.	Roper Industries, Inc.	Stepan Co.
Pfizer Inc.	Rouse Co.	Sterling Bancshares, Inc.
Piedmont Natural Gas Co., Inc.	RPM International Inc.	Sterling Financial Corp.
Pier 1 Imports Inc.	S & T Bancorp, Inc.	Stryker Corp.

Table 7.4 Mergent Dividend Achievers 2004 (cont'd.)

SunTrust Banks, Inc.	United Mobile Homes, Inc.	WestAmerica Bancorporation
Superior Industries International, Inc.	United Technologies Corp.	Weyco Group, Inc.
Supervalu Inc.	Universal Corp.	WGL Holdings, Inc.
Susquehanna Bancshares, Inc.	Universal Health Realty Income Trust	Whitney Holding Corp.
SWS Group, Inc.	Unizan Financial Corp.	Wiley (John) & Sons Inc.
Synovus Financial Corp.	Valley National Bancorp	Wilmington Trust Corp.
Sysco Corp.	Valspar Corp.	Wolverine World Wide, Inc.
T Rowe Price Group Inc.	Vectren Corp	WPS Resources Corp.
Tanger Factory Outlet Centers, Inc.	VF Corp.	Wrigley (William) Jr. Co.
Target Corp.	Vulcan Materials Co.	
TCF Financial Corp.	Walgreen Co.	
Teleflex Incorporated	Wal-Mart Stores, Inc.	
Telephone and Data Systems, Inc.	Washington Federal Inc.	
Tennant Co.	Washington Mutual Inc.	
TEPPCO Partners, L.P.	Washington Real Estate Investment Trust	
Tootsie Roll Industries Inc.	Webster Financial Corp.	
Transatlantic Holdings, Inc.	Weingarten Realty Investors	
Trustmark Corp.	Wells Fargo & Co.	
UGI Corp.	Wesbanco, Inc.	
United Bankshares, Inc.	Wesco Financial Corp.	
United Dominion Realty Trust, Inc.	West Pharmaceutical Services, Inc.	

For most of us, this is way too many stocks to purchase. For starters, buying 100 shares of each of these 303 stocks would cost more than a million dollars. Even if you bought them all, their yield was still only 2.7 percent in 2003—nothing to get excited about. Remember: These companies are only celebrated for consistently raising their dividends, not for paying the highest dividends.

Enter the investment management company BlackRock. This organization has licensed the index and uses it as the basis for the two closed-end mutual funds listed in Table 7.2 (see page 95).

The BlackRock Dividend Achievers Trust (BDV) takes 60 to 80 of the top-yielding stocks from the Mergent Dividend Achievers and buys them. By focusing only on the highest-yielding stocks from the list, the yield on this fund can be significantly higher than the Mergent index as a whole (a 6 percent total return is its aim).

The BlackRock Strategic Dividend Achievers Trust (BDT) takes the highest-yielding small- and mid-cap stocks from the Mergent Dividend Achievers and invests in these. The thinking here is that the world of dividend stocks is sufficiently large that it's possible to usefully "slice and dice" it for further diversification. It, too, hopes to deliver a 6 percent total return.

Please remain seated: *This is not necessarily a 6 percent dividend yield.* BlackRock intends to provide this payment come rain or shine, so if the market sinks and the funds don't have sufficient reserves to pay shareholders from their dividends or capital gains, they'll dip into principal. In other words, they'd pay you the distribution out of the money you handed to them to invest in the first place. In the normal course of events, though, the monthly payment would include a mixture of dividends and capital gains—some of which would likely be short-term capital gains taxed as ordinary income, if held in a taxable account. Some of this income would be from real estate investment trusts, which might comprise about 10 percent of these funds (also largely taxable as ordinary income). Since these funds aren't designed to exactly track the Mergent index, they may also trade at a significant premium or discount to the underlying value of their assets. This also distinguishes them from iShare's DVY, which, being an exchange traded index fund rather than a closed-end fund, should closely follow the Dow Jones Select Dividend Index.

The Standard & Poor's Dividend Aristocrats

Standard & Poor's is also in the dividend-stock-tracking game. Their Dividend Aristocrats include the companies within the S&P 500 Index that have paid increasing dividends over each of the past 25 years—a full quarter century. The latest list is provided in Table 7.5.

Table 7.5: Standard & Poor's Dividend Aristocrats 09/2004			
Company	**Ticker**	**Yield**	**Industry**
3M Co.	MMM	1.8%	Industrials
Abbott Laboratories	ABT	2.5%	Health Care
ALLTEL Corp.	AT	2.7%	Communication
Altria Group	MO	6.2%	Consumer
AmSouth Bancorp	ASO	3.9%	Financials
Anheuser-Busch Cos.	BUD	2.0%	Consumer
Archer Daniels Midland	ADM	1.8%	Consumer
Automatic Data Proc.	ADP	1.4%	Technology
Avery Dennison Corp.	AVY	2.3%	Industrials
Bank of America	BAC	4.2%	Financials
Bard (C.R.)	BCR	0.9%	Health Care
Becton, Dickinson	BDX	1.2%	Health Care
CenturyTel Inc.	CTL	0.7%	Communication
Chubb Corp.	CB	2.2%	Financials
Clorox Co.	CLX	2.0%	Consumer
Coca-Cola Co.	KO	2.5%	Consumer
Comerica Inc.	CMA	3.5%	Financials
ConAgra Foods	CAG	4.2%	Consumer
Consolidated Edison	ED	5.4%	Utilities
Donnelley (R.R.) & Sons	RRD	3.3%	Industrials
Dover Corp.	DOV	1.7%	Industrials
Emerson Electric	EMR	2.6%	Industrials
Family Dollar Stores	FDO	1.3%	Consumer
First Horizon Natl.	FHN	3.7%	Financials
Gannett Co.	GCI	1.3%	Consumer
Genl. Electric	GE	2.4%	Industrials

Table 7.5: Standard & Poor's Dividend Aristocrats (cont'd.)			
Company	Ticker	Yield	Industry
Grainger (W.W.)	GWW	1.4%	Industrials
Jefferson-Pilot	JP	3.1%	Financials
Johnson & Johnson	JNJ	2.0%	Health Care
Johnson Controls	JCI	1.6%	Consumer
KeyCorp	KEY	3.9%	Financials
Kimberly-Clark	KMB	2.5%	Consumer
Leggett & Platt	LEG	2.1%	Consumer
Lilly (Eli)	LLY	2.4%	Health Care
Lowe's Cos.	LOW	0.3%	Consumer
Marsh & McLennan	MMC	3.0%	Financials
Masco Corp.	MAS	2.1%	Industrials
May Dept Stores	MAY	3.8%	Consumer
McDonald's Corp.	MCD	2.0%	Consumer
McGraw-Hill Companies	MHP	1.5%	Consumer
Merck & Co.	MRK	4.6%	Health Care
Nucor Corp.	NUE	1.1%	Materials
PepsiCo Inc.	PEP	1.9%	Consumer
Pfizer, Inc.	PFE	2.2%	Health Care
PPG Indus.	PPG	2.9%	Materials
Procter & Gamble	PG	1.9%	Consumer
Regions Financial	RF	4.0%	Financials
Rohm & Haas	ROH	2.3%	Materials
Sigma-Aldrich	SIAL	1.2%	Materials
SouthTrust Corp.	SOTR	2.3%	Financials
Stanley Works	SWK	2.6%	Consumer
Supervalu Inc.	SVU	2.2%	Consumer
Sysco Corp.	SYY	1.7%	Consumer
Target Corp.	TGT	0.7%	Consumer
U.S. Bancorp	USB	3.3%	Financials
VF Corp.	VFC	2.1%	Consumer
Wal-Mart Stores	WMT	1.0%	Consumer
Walgreen Co.	WAG	0.6%	Consumer

The Standard & Poor's list is similar to the Mergent list, except that its stocks have a 25-year pedigree instead of ten years, and it makes no demands upon the companies' trading volumes. In fact, nearly every stock on the more demanding Standard & Poor's list is on the Mergent list. There's just one problem: The average dividend yield of these 58 stocks is 2.4 percent as of this writing—hardly the stuff of retirement dreams, even if those dividends are likely to increase every year. As with the Mergent list, these are consistent dividend raisers, not necessarily the highest payers. If you wanted to own them, you'd find that there's no convenient fund that samples all 58 stocks, so you'd have to buy them one by one.

From the income investor's point of view, focusing on stocks that consistently raise their dividends is a suboptimal strategy. Robert Arnott (editor of the *Financial Analysts Journal*) has pointed out that, over the past 200 years, the real growth in dividends has contributed only 0.8 percent of the stock market's annualized total real return, compared with the 5 percent contributed by the dividends themselves. Dividend investors are better off picking the stocks that are actually paying good dividends, not the ones that are raising them.

Are Two (or Three) Heads Better than One?

Ultimately, we want the best of both worlds: high dividend payers and also consistent dividend raisers. The trick might be to combine two lists: the Dow Jones Select Dividend List (the high payers) with the Mergent Dividend Achievers (the long-term payers and raisers) or the Standard & Poor's Dividend Aristocrats (the super-long-term payers and raisers). Table 7.6 includes a list of the 24 stocks that are switch-hitters on the Dow Jones and Mergent lists as of this writing—the ones that made the cut on both teams. (Be aware that the list may be different by the time you read this.)

Table 7.6: Dow Jones/Mergent Crossovers 09/2004			
Name	Ticker	Yield	Industry
Altria Group Inc.	MO	6.3%	Tobacco
AmSouth Bancorp	ASO	3.9%	Banks
Associated Banc-Corp.	ASBC	3.1%	Banks
Bank of America Corp.	BAC	4.1%	Banks
Black Hills Corp.	BKH	4.5%	Electric Utilities
Citizens Banking Corp.	CBCF	3.5%	Banks
Comerica Inc.	CMA	3.5%	Banks
FirstMerit Corp.	FMER	4.1%	Banks
Genuine Parts Co.	GPC	3.2%	Auto Parts
Hibernia Corp.	HIB	3.1%	Banks
Hudson United Bancorp	HU	3.8%	Banks
KeyCorp	KEY	4.0%	Banks
Lincoln National Corp.	LNC	3.0%	Insurance
National City Corp.	NCC	3.6%	Banks
Nicor Inc.	GAS	5.1%	Gas Utilities
People's Bank	PBCT	3.3%	Banks
Pinnacle West Capital	PNW	4.4%	Electric Utilities
PPG Industries Inc.	PPG	2.9%	Chemicals
RPM International Inc.	RPM	3.3%	Chemicals
SBC Communications Inc.	SBC	4.8%	Communications
Sonoco Products Co.	SON	3.3%	Packaging
Universal Corp.	UVV	3.5%	Tobacco
Washington Federal Inc.	WFSL	3.4%	Savings & Loan
Whitney Holding Corp.	WTNY	3.2%	Banks

You could buy 100 shares of each of these 24 stocks for $88,189 today and earn a respectable yield of 3.8 percent—a bit better than that of the iShares Dow Jones index and without the ongoing management fees (but with a portfolio that needs some consistent supervision on your part).

Not a bad way to go—our only complaint is that this list is top-heavy in stocks from the financial sector. You could always cut back your holdings from these, perhaps only buying a representative sampling. It has possibilities.

Table 7.7 shows a much shorter list of stocks that made it on both the Dow Jones Select Dividend list as well as on the Standard & Poor's Dividend Aristocrat list.

Table 7.7: Dow Jones/S&P Crossovers 09/2004			
Name	**Ticker**	**Yield**	**Industry**
Altria Group	MO	6.3%	Consumer
AmSouth Bancorp	ASO	3.9%	Financials
Bank of America	BAC	3.9%	Financials
Comerica Inc.	CMA	3.5%	Financials
Donnelley (R.R.) & Sons	RRD	3.3%	Industrials
KeyCorp	KEY	4.0%	Financials
PPG Indus.	PPG	2.9%	Materials

While the resulting stocks have a 4.0 percent dividend yield as of this writing, they make for an unbalanced portfolio, tilted way toward the financial sector, just as the Mergent/Dow Jones crossover list was.

The Stein-DeMuth Dividend Stock Short List

The situation seemed to us to call for some further thinking. We retired to the club, filled our calabash pipes with shag, and decanted a bottle of port. Here is what emerged:

1. There's no point in buying any individual stock whose yield is less than that of iShares' DVY fund. Why take on the individual business risk unless you're being paid a higher yield to compensate for it? This immediately eliminates a huge number of dividend stocks from consideration.

2. If you're buying individual stocks, you still need diversification. A 20-stock portfolio is hardly diversified if it's composed entirely of electric utilities or regional banks.

3. You can't ignore fundamentals. It doesn't do you any good to buy a company that pays a whopping dividend if that yield is in danger because the corporation is paying out more than it's earning, or if it's about to go bankrupt. If something sounds too good to be true, it probably is. You want to eliminate those companies that, for whatever reason, have been paying a *faux*, unsustainably high dividend.

4. While Mergent and Standard & Poor's list companies that raise their dividends annually, your concerns are likely more modest: You want companies that pay dividends regularly and consistently, never cutting or omitting them. You want *steady payers*, even if they're only occasional dividend *raisers*. You're looking for the dividend increases to keep up with (or surpass) inflation over time. They don't need to rise every year, so long as when they do increase, they keep you even in terms of purchasing power. Since you'd be buying a number of companies, at least some of them would probably be raising their dividends during any given year, keeping you in purchasing-power parity.

5. These dividend indexes typically limit their lists to high-volume, liquid stocks in order to be useful to institutional investors who might buy or sell tens of thousands of shares per day. This isn't an issue for small-time individual investors. As long as a stock is publicly traded on a national exchange, that's good enough for those of us sitting in the peanut gallery. You can consider buying smaller companies with lower trading volumes than the ones the big boys at Dow Jones and Mergent are hunting.

With this in mind, we assembled two dividend stock portfolios: a diversified one and a minimalist one.

Table 7.8: A Diversified Dividend Stock Portfolio 09/2004

Shares	Price	Stock	Ticker	Yield
500s	$28,700	*iShares DJ Select Div. Index*	DVY	3.3%
100s	$4,615	*Ameren*	AEE	5.5%
100s	$2,998	*Southern*	SO	4.7%
100s	$4,168	*Peoples Energy*	PGL	5.2%
100s	$2,833	*National Fuel Gas*	NFG	3.9%
100s	$2,595	*SBC Communications*	SBC	4.7%
100s	$1,282	*TrustCo*	TRST	4.7%
100s	$3,908	*Washington Mutual*	WM	4.4%
100s	$4,157	*Unitrin*	UTR	4.0%
100s	$2,784	*ConAgra*	CAG	4.1%
100s	$4,102	*Deluxe*	DLX	3.6%

This portfolio costs about $62,000 and generates 3.9 percent yield. As you'll see in Chapter 12, an allocation of this amount purely to dividend stocks implies that you have about $300,000 to spend on your income portfolio in total. To give an idea of risk, during the interest rate uncertainties of April 2004, this selection of dividend stocks was down 2.9 percent.

Table 7.9 shows a minimalist version of the same portfolio.

Table 7.9: A Minimum Dividend Stock Portfolio 09/2004

Shares	Price	Stock	Ticker	Yield
250s	$14,350	*iShares DJ Select Div. Index*	DVY	3.3%
100s	$4,615	*Ameren*	AEE	5.5%
100s	$2,833	*National Fuel Gas*	NFG	3.9%
100s	$2,387	*SBC Communications*	SBC	5.3%
100s	$1,286	*TrustCo Bank*	TRST	4.7%
100s	$4,157	*Unitrin*	UTR	4.0%

This portfolio generates 4.0 percent in annual yield—0.75 percentage points higher than DVY by itself, and slightly more than the more diversified portfolio (a trade-off of more yield for less diversification—and presumably less safety—it was down 3.4 percent in April 2004). Currently, this group of stocks would cost about $30,000, which, as you'll see, implies total investment assets of about $150,000 for your total income portfolio. If you don't have enough money to buy the stocks in the minimal portfolio, then you should put the money you earmark for dividend stocks in the Dow Jones Select Dividend Index and leave it at that.

One problem with stock "buy" lists like these is that they tend to have the shelf life of an egg salad sandwich. They may be out-of-date by the time you read this. We've picked companies that we think are strong long-term contenders, but we don't have a Ouija board. In case the unexpected happens, we want to equip you to make your own selection of dividend stocks.

Tables 7.10 through 7.13 list companies that have been selected from four dividend-friendly sectors of the economy: finance, utilities, consumer products, and industry. At the time of this writing, any of these companies might be a candidate for a dividend investor, but by the time you read this, things may have changed. A company's price may have risen, causing its dividend yield to fall, or the company may have been beset by hard times. For this reason, instead of only suggesting a definitive dividend portfolio that might be out-of-date, we want to give you a very short list of stocks that merit your further research, and then tell you exactly what to look for. Not surprisingly, many of the other companies on our lists are also on the all-star dividend lists we've already reviewed. Our lists should be good starting points, but they are by no means exhaustive.

Table 7.10: Financial Sector Dividend Stocks 09/2004

Company	Ticker	Yield	Industry
AmSouth Bancorporation	ASO	3.9%	Banking
Bank of America	BAC	3.8%	Banking
Barclays ADR	BCS	4.0%	Banking
BB&T	BBT	3.3%	Banking
Comerica	CMA	3.5%	Banking
FirstMerit	FMER	4.0%	Banking
KeyCorp	KEY	3.9%	Banking
National City	NCC	3.4%	Banking
Regions Financial	RF	4.0%	Banking
Susquehanna Bancshares	SUSQ	3.6%	Banking
TrustCo Bank Corporation of NY	TRST	4.7%	Banking
Unitrin	UTR	4.0%	Insurance
Washington Federal	WFSL	3.2%	S & L

Table 7.11: Utility Sector Dividend Stocks

Name	Ticker	Yield	Utility
Allete	ALE	10.4%	Electric
Ameren	AEE	5.5%	Electric
Black Hills	BKH	4.4%	Electric
Cinergy	CIN	4.7%	Electric
Consolidated Edison	ED	5.4%	Electric
DTE Energy Holding	DTE	4.9%	Electric
FPL Group	FPL	3.7%	Electric
Great Plains Energy	GXP	5.7%	Electric
MGE Energy	MGEE	4.3%	Electric
OGE Energy Corp	OGE	5.3%	Electric
Otter Tail	OTTR	4.3%	Electric
Pinnacle West	PNW	4.3%	Electric
Progress Energy	PGN	5.4%	Electric
Southern	SO	4.7%	Electric
Atmos Energy	ATO	4.8%	Gas
Chesapeake Utilities	CPK	4.4%	Gas
Nicor	GAS	5.1%	Gas
National Fuel Gas	NFG	3.9%	Gas
Peoples Energy	PGL	5.2%	Gas
Piedmont Natural Gas	PNY	3.9%	Gas
UGI	UGI	3.2%	Gas
WGL Holdings	WGL	4.6%	Gas
SBC Communications	SBC	4.7%	Telephone
Verizon Communications	VZ	3.9%	Telephone

Table 7.12: Consumer Sector Dividend Stocks

Name	Ticker	Yield	Industry Group
Altria Group	MO	5.9%	Tobacco
Bristol-Myers Squibb	BMY	5.9%	Medical
ConAgra Foods	CAG	4.1%	Food & Beverage
Genuine Parts	GPC	3.1%	Retail
Heinz HJ	HNZ	3.1%	Food & Beverage
May Department Stores	MAY	3.8%	Retail
Merck	MRK	4.5%	Medical
Sara Lee	SLE	3.3%	Food & Beverage
Sonoco Products	SON	3.3%	Packaging
Superior Uniform Group	SGC	3.9%	Apparel
Universal	UVV	3.4%	Tobacco
UST	UST	5.1%	Tobacco

Table 7.13: Business & Industrial Dividend Stocks

Name	Ticker	Yield	Industry
Bandag	BDG	3.0%	Soft Commodities
ChevronTexaco	CVX	2.8%	Oil & Gas
Deluxe	DLX	3.6%	Commercial Services
DuPont	DD	3.3%	Chemicals
Landauer	LDR	3.4%	Commercial Services
Quaker Chemical	KWR	3.5%	Oil & Gas
RR Donnelley	RRD	3.3%	Commercial Services
Southern Peru Copper	PCU	3.5%	Mining
Standard Register	SR	8.8%	Commercial Services
Worthington Industries	WOR	3.0%	Hard Commodities

Here's how we recommend making your own individual stock selections from these lists:

1. Go to **www.morningstar.com** and look up the trailing 12-month dividend yield of iShare's Dow Jones Select Dividend Index Fund (ticker: DVY). Yahoo! Finance, MSN, and any number of other places on the Web also list it, but remember that different sites may have different ways of calculating the yield. Since you'll be getting further information from Morningstar (which uses the trailing 12-month's dividend yield), it's easiest to start there. The DVY yield is your benchmark.

2. Armed with this information, you know the yield to beat. Punch in the tickers from the companies above, and note which ones have an appreciably higher yield than DVY.

3. Then, like ordering from a take-out menu, select several stocks from each table that appear promising, and enter their tickers into Morningstar for a closer look.

    a. Using Morningstar's "Snapshot" page for each company, see if your choice is profitable and in reasonable financial health by checking the grades Morningstar gives it. (Remember, these aren't "growth" companies, so you can ignore that factor, even if it gets an "F.")

    b. Then, going to Morningstar's "Charts and Returns" page (the tab is on the left-hand column), look down the page at the stock's dividend history for the past few years. Has the dividend been cut for any reason recently? If so, cross that stock off your list.

4. You'll probably want to buy several utilities and banks. Even here, diversification can help. Try to find companies in different areas of the country. If the gas utility you select serves Houston, buy an electric utility that powers Seattle. The idea is to spread your bets. Also, companies with a larger market capitalization tend to be more stable than smaller companies, which may be important if you're buying a minimalist portfolio.

5. Finally, keep in mind that the consumer, business, and industrial stocks are generally going to have lower yields than those of the banks and utilities, and they may be only slightly higher than the yield offered by DVY. Where their yields are notably higher, they may be clustered in one industry (such as tobacco) where there's a large amount of business (not to mention cancer and heart-disease) risk.

If you're planning to use a diversified investment vehicle like DVY as the core of your dividend portfolio, there's no need to buy any of these, since they're already well represented. However, because some investors might want to assemble their dividend portfolio entirely of individual stocks, we present these companies as candidates. Diversification across industry groups is always desirable.

Following this procedure, your final dividend portfolio might look like Table 7.14:

Table 7.14: A Diversified Dividend Stock Portfolio

Name	Ticker	Allocation
iShares Dow Jones Select Dividend	DVY	50%
Electric Utility #1		
Electric Utility #2		
Gas Utility #1		
Gas Utility #2		All
Telephone Utility		Combined
Financial #1		50%
Financial #2		
Other Dividend Stock		
Other Dividend Stock		
Other Dividend Stock		

There's nothing cast in concrete about this allocation. The big idea here is to use DVY as the core of your dividend stock strategy and then add a number of stocks with higher dividend yields to supplement it and turbocharge the yield. Since you're buying stocks rather than shares of mutual funds, it will be to your advantage to buy these in round lots of 100 (or some multiple thereof).

The minimalist portfolio would resemble the one shown in Table 7.15:

Table 7.15: A Minimum Dividend Stock Portfolio

Name	Ticker	Allocation
iShares Dow Jones Select Dividend	DVY	50%
Electric Utility		
Gas Utility		All
Telephone Utility		Combined
Bank		50%
Other Dividend Stock		

To recap: Let iShare's DVY do the heavy lifting for your dividend-stock portfolio and then round it out with some choice additions.

Next, there's another class of income-intensive securities in the stock kingdom to be aware of: preferred stock.

████

CHAPTER EIGHT

Preferred Stock

Preferred stock is a security that has several peculiar features. It's called *preferred* because preferred shareholders stand in line ahead of common shareholders when the time comes to pay dividends, and ahead of them once more in the unhappy event that the company liquidates. Preferred stock can be complicated, but resolute fixed-income investors should pay attention.

Preferred stock is most often issued at $50 or $100 par (making a round lot of 100 shares affordable at $5,000 or $10,000) with a *fixed* dividend. Unlike common shares of stock (which may or may not pay a dividend, and which dividends may fluctuate with the company's earnings), preferred shares propose to pay the same dividend, the same dollar amount, year after year. Often issued by banks, insurance companies, and utility companies, they're among the very highest-yielding investments.

Of course, there's no *guarantee* that investors will receive the dividend. For example, a company's board of directors can vote to suspend the dividend indefinitely. (Such an action may trigger the acquisition of voting rights by preferred stockholders, which they normally don't have.) If and when the time comes to resume payments, not only will preferred stockholders be paid first, in most cases they'll be paid any back dividends owed as well. These are called *cumulative preferreds*, since the dividends accumulate even when unpaid.

Historically, the main buyers of preferred stock have been other corporations. This is because of a tax loophole that allows class "C" corporations to collect 70 percent of the dividends from preferred stock tax-free, while they must pay taxes on 100 percent of the bond income they receive.

Alas, the same tax break is not available to individuals. This by itself would seem to invalidate this group of securities from further consideration, since you'd be stuck collecting a lower yield on fairly illiquid securities while corporations got all the benefit. But in 1993, new classes of preferred stock began to be issued that are fully taxable to all parties—and which pay higher yields to compensate. This leveled the playing field. These preferreds are in some ways like bonds, in that they're based on earnings from a trust created by the corporation. As a result, their dividends aren't taxed at the lower Bush-dividend rates applicable to ordinary common stock dividends.

Interest in preferreds has grown as the market has opened to individual investors. These new "trust" preferreds are sold on stock exchanges at $25 par value, making them much more accessible than corporate bonds, which sell on the bond market at $1,000 apiece. Their yields are slightly higher than those of similar corporate bonds because of their secondary status in the event of liquidation and their lack of a promise of return of principal.

After preferred shares are issued, they trade in the market like any other negotiable security. While the price of a company's common stock will vary with the company's fortunes, the preferred stock generally won't, since theoretically the preferred shareholder continues to receive the same fixed dividend or interest no matter what the company's fate (short of some disaster). This means that the price of preferred shares varies with the changes in the interest-rate environment, just as bonds' prices do. A share of preferred stock can be thought of as a long-term (one hopes, perpetual) bond that never matures. When long-term rates drop, the price of preferred stock will increase significantly; when long-term rates rise, the price will fall.

Preferred stocks have several other bondlike features, and they're even rated by the same agencies that evaluate bonds. Nowadays, almost all new issues are *callable preferreds*, where management has the privilege of calling in the securities after a set date. This changes their complexion significantly, as management can pay off the stock if interest rates drop (precisely the situation in which the preferred shareholder wishes to maintain the higher yield).

If you pay $55 per share for a preferred stock that management calls a few years from now at a par value of $50, the $5-per-share loss you take has to be weighed against the dividends you'll receive. This could cut your effective yield considerably, although until this day comes (and it may never arrive), preferreds pay a higher yield to compensate investors for taking this call risk.

There can also be *convertible preferreds*, where preferred shareholders have the right to convert their preferred shares into common stock under certain conditions. Still other preferreds are *participating*, which is to say they benefit from any extra dividends that the board of directors declares for common investors. There are even preferreds that pay variable dividends, usually benchmarked in some specified way to the Treasury yield curve.

Here are more issues to consider:

- The same company may issue different classes of preferred stock with different characteristics at different times. The presence of the various embedded options makes the securities difficult to analyze and price.

- Again, many of the post-1993 shares floating around out there aren't true preferreds, but "trust" shares that basically own debt and whose dividends are treated as taxable interest (think *your marginal tax rate*) rather than ordinary dividends (think *15 percent tax rate*).

- The marketplace for preferreds is similar to that for corporate bonds. Only the larger and better rated issues trade efficiently. About half of preferred stocks trade over the counter, where pricing is impressionistic and trading becomes expensive.

To examine several thousand preferred securities with all their bewildering features, the place to go on the Internet is **www. quantumonline.com**.

Table 8.1 gives a list of some true preferreds that we believe will qualify for the new 15 percent tax treatment. These have at least an "A" level credit rating from Moody's or Standard & Poor's as of this writing, have call dates a few years out, and trade on the New York Stock Exchange (where pricing should be efficient). Note that all of them have a higher yield than our diversified stock dividend portfolio, so they're intended for aggressive income investors.

The ticker symbols vary from place to place, so investors interested in purchasing individual preferred securities should consult the primer on this topic at the Quantum Website. (We warned you this wasn't easy!)

Table 8.1: Preferred Securities 09/2004

Security	Cusip	Dividend	Yield	Call Date
ABN Amro Capital Funding V, 5.90% Noncum. Guar. Trust	00372P203	$1.48	6.3%	7/3/08
ABN Amro Capital Funding VI, 6.25% Noncum. Guar. Trust	00080V203	$1.56	6.3%	9/30/08
ABN Amro Capital Funding VII, 6.08% Noncum. Guar. Trust	0037Q201	$1.52	6.3%	2/18/09
Bear Stearns Companies, 5.49% Dep Cumul. Pfd. Stock G	73902868	$2.75	5.4%	7/15/08
Fannie Mae, 5.50% Non-Cumul. Preferred Stock, Series N	313586828	$2.75	5.8%	9/25/08
Freddie Mac, 5.81% Perpetual Non-cum. Preferred Stock	313400772	$2.91	5.7%	3/31/11
Freddie Mac, 5.79% Perpetual Non-cum. Preferred Stock	313400830	$2.90	5.7%	6/30/09
Gabelli Equity Trust, 5.875% Cumul. Preferred Stock D	362397705	$1.47	5.8%	9/26/08
Gabelli Utility Trust, Inc., 5.625% Cumul. Pfd. Shares A	36240A200	$1.41	5.6%	7/31/08
General American Investors, 5.95% Cumul. Pfd. Stock B	368802401	$1.49	6.0%	9/24/08
ING Groep NV Perpetual Debt Securities	456837400	$1.55	6.3%	1/15/09
Lehman Brothers Holdings, 5.67% Dep Shares Pfd. Stock D	524908886	$2.84	5.7%	8/31/08
Mississippi Power 5.25% Series Dep Shares Cum. Preferred	605417773	$1.31	5.4%	4/7/09
Royce Focus Trust Inc., 6.00% Cumulative Preferred Stock	78080N306	$1.50	6.0%	10/17/08
Royce Micro-Cap Trust, 6.00% Cumulative Preferred Stock	780915302	$1.50	6.0%	10/16/08

Today, you can buy 100 shares of each of the 15 companies in Table 8.1 for about $50,000. You lock in your dividend at the time of purchase, at least until the call date. These should be like a small cup of sorbet to an income portfolio, rather than an entrée. Keep in mind the following:

- Prices will fluctuate with interest rates (and credit ratings), so for the most part, you can ignore the price variations and deposit the dividend checks, which is the reason you bought them in the first place.

- The average yield of a portfolio consisting of 100 shares each of these true preferreds is currently 5.9 percent.

To recap: Preferred stock should do well in the same investment environments where long-term bonds succeed. They represent a different asset class and so offer some diversification with a decided tax advantage over bond income. They also carry higher risks than long-term bonds: The dividend is less certain, there's no promised return of principal, and preferred shareholders line up behind bondholders for any proceeds should the company be forced to liquidate.

Leveraged Closed-End Dividend Funds

If picking preferred stocks seems tricky (and it is), you could leave the selection up to fund managers and pay them to select preferreds on your behalf. These preferred-stock mutual funds are typically closed-end: The fund managers buy and sell securities within the closed-end fund wrapper, immune from hot money entering and leaving, which could completely distort prices in a thinly traded market like that of preferreds.

Although this closed-end format works better, it also introduces the risks of leverage, since all the closed-end preferred-stock funds are also leveraged funds. The lower the short-term rates are, the better these funds should perform. If short-term rates rise, however, the gap between borrowing costs and what the preferreds pay can narrow or close, and then these funds will be in trouble.

While owning a single preferred stock should give you the same dividend payout year after year, owning a fund of preferred stocks will provide a payout that varies over time, as preferreds are called or sold and have to be replaced with new issues that reflect present interest-rate realities. With dividend stocks, you looked for a ten-year history of rising dividends, but preferred-stock funds can't offer this since they march to a different beat: the jungle drum of interest rates.

Table 8.2 shows a list of some closed-end leveraged funds investing in preferred stocks. (They also invest in bonds and utility stocks, so they aren't a pure play.)

Table 8.2 Preferred Dividend Funds 09/2004			
Fund	**Ticker**	**Yield**	**Expense**
BlackRock Pref. Opportunity Trust	BPP	7.8%	1.5%
DNP Select Income	DNP	9.8%	1.9%
F&C/Claymore Preferred Securities	FFC	8.2%	1.0%
John Hancock Preferred Equity Inc.	HPI	8.5%	1.0%
John Hancock Preferred Income 2	HPF	8.5%	1.0%
John Hancock Preferred Income 3	HPS	9.3%	1.1%
Nuveen Quality Preferred Income	JTP	8.4%	1.9%
Nuveen Quality Preferred Income 2	JPS	7.9%	1.5%
Nuveen Quality Preferred Income 3	JHP	8.1%	1.5%
Preferred Income Fund	PFD	7.5%	1.5%
Preferred Income Opportunity Fund	PFO	7.5%	1.5%
Preferred Income Strategies Fund	PSY	8.9%	1.1%

What's more, the preferreds they invest in include both types of preferred stock—those that issue real preferred dividends, as well as preferred trusts paying interest that's fully taxable as ordinary income. You'll find out how much of each at the end of the year, when the funds send out the tax breakdown to shareholders.

This factor definitely shouldn't be ignored. The average yield of the high-quality preferreds in Table 8.1 is 5.9 percent, while the average dividend yield of the leveraged preferred funds is currently 8.4 percent. *If the leveraged preferred fund pays all its dividends from trusts rather than true preferred stock, the after-tax advantage shrinks to less than half a percentage point for taxpayers in the 35 percent bracket.*

As of today, the Nuveen funds are invested almost entirely in the hybrid, taxable preferreds, and the John Hancock funds have 80 percent of their assets in these fully taxable securities. For this reason, investors seeking the higher returns from leverage would be better advised to hold these types of funds in a tax-deferred account. At that point, however, they compete head-to-head with long-term bonds, which can offer higher credit quality.

What's the solution? Table 8.3 offers a list of some closed-end leveraged funds (all from John Hancock) that invest in preferred as well as ordinary dividend stocks. Their yield is taxable entirely at the lower-dividend rate, and so they fit comfortably into a taxable account.

Table 8.3: Leveraged Tax-Friendly Dividend Funds 09/2004			
Fund	Ticker	Yield	Expense
John Hancock Patriot Premium Div.	PDF	7.8%	1.9%
John Hancock Patriot Premium Div. 2	PDT	7.1%	1.9%
John Hancock Patriot Select	DIV	7.7%	1.7%
John Hancock Patriot Global	PGD	7.3%	1.9%
John Hancock Patriot Preferred	PPF	8.2%	1.9%

These funds have all the risks and advantages that leveraging brings. Their day-to-day price can be expected to fluctuate even more than that of an unleveraged preferred, which may not bother you as long as you're getting a steady and enhanced dividend check.

Here's the reality check: During April of 2004, the John Hancock Patriot Premium Dividend fund (PDF) was down nearly 11 percent. By comparison, our preferreds in Table 8.1 were down closer to 4 percent, reflecting their shorter maturities as well as the absence of leverage.

Should the yield curve invert and the fund managers fail to get out of the way, you could receive less interest from the fund than simply from owning an unleveraged bundle of preferred stocks. In that event, the discount at which the fund sells would increase sharply, and you'd risk taking a significant loss if you were to sell at such a time.

Aggressive income investors with the constitution for the uncertainties inherent in these investments could consider one of these funds for a portion of their income portfolios held in taxable accounts. There are uncertainties in price, but the yields are enticing.

Now we turn to an essential part of the high-income investor's equity toolbox: the real estate investment trust.

CHAPTER NINE

Real Estate Investment Trusts

Notice all those buildings you see as you walk down the street? Somebody owns them. Often, they belong to the company whose name is on the door, but in other cases, they can belong to something called a *real estate investment trust (REIT)*. An equity REIT owns physical property: skyscrapers, malls, hospitals, hotels, shopping centers, nursing homes, and the like. In fact, these trusts presently own about 10 to 15 percent of all commercial real estate in the United States.

In addition to owning properties, a REIT also manages them. It leases space, screens tenants, collects the rent, renovates, paints, patches, carpets, and fixes the water heater and air conditioning—doing whatever it takes to keep the properties operational. It manages a portfolio of real estate, selling existing properties and buying new ones as it deems advantageous.

REITs shouldn't be confused with their bastard stepparents from hell: the real estate limited partnerships of the 1980s. These partnerships were sold as tax shelters, and since the value of the tax dodge was far greater than the property itself, they played havoc with real estate markets all over the country. Fees were based on the value of all properties held, giving management a tremendous incentive to go on buying sprees. They were also illiquid, or at least semi-illiquid: They were easy to buy but nearly impossible to sell. They finally disappeared when the IRS plugged the tax loophole. The novel 'Ludes, by one of your authors, Ben Stein, chronicled the downfall of this operation (James Woods starred in the movie version, which was called *The Boost*).

Why should you own shares in a REIT? If you own your home, and that's already your biggest single asset, why would you want to put even more money into real estate?

Here's the reason: Residential and commercial real estate are two distinct asset classes whose fortunes are not necessarily correlated. There are two problems with a house when considered as an asset: It's undiversified, and it's illiquid. By undiversified, we mean that it participates solely in the local market. If the big factory in town closes, your home's value might plummet. This makes it riskier than if you owned houses in a number of different towns, as polygamists and movie stars do.

To be fair, saying a house is "illiquid" is something of a misnomer—you *could* sell your house this afternoon, if pressed. However, you'd probably have to accept considerably less than full market price for the place. It might take weeks or months to obtain a fair price, and the transaction costs would be steep—6 percent is typical.

Real estate investment trusts solve both these problems. Since a REIT is a collection of properties that are often located in diverse geographic regions, by buying several REITs you can cover the giant green baccarat table that is the economic landscape of the United States. With REITs, you can own a stake in a nationally diversified portfolio of commercial real estate properties with as little as $100.

Since REITs trade on stock exchanges, shares can be bought and sold within ten seconds any time the market is open, whereas an individual rental property might take months to unload if the neighborhood has gone downhill. You can sell a million dollars' worth of stock in a REIT mutual fund for a commission of $10; on the other hand, if you sell a single million-dollar rental property, your broker may want a bit more—like $59,990 more.

REITs also have other advantages over purchasing rental property. Although both use leverage to supplement their return, REITs are only leveraged at about 50 percent. If you were to buy a rental, you might put down a mere 20 percent and therefore leverage 80 percent. But you could equalize the amount of leverage by buying REITs on margin or in a leveraged closed-end mutual fund (which we'll tell you more about in a moment).

When you compare the yields on REITs to those from owning the apartment house of your dreams, you'll find they're not far apart. What you give up is the joy of dealing with tenants. You might think that tenants will be grateful for being provided with a place to live, and so will take excellent care of your property, always paying the rent on time and never giving you any trouble. Occasionally, however, one may present a peccadillo.

One of your authors ruefully recalls how, during his dissipated and misspent youth, he dressed up in a suit and tie to present himself with utter politesse to a persnickety, arthritic landlady. Then, having insinuated himself in the new digs, friends from the Fillmore West theater came to visit on the very first weekend, hauling in crates of equipment from their truck and putting on an industrial-strength light-and-sound show in the living room (but really entertaining the whole building) that can only be described as "psychedelic."

Then there was the problem with the water bed. Running the hose through the second-story window and inserting it into the mattress, your author went outside, turned on the spigot, and smoked a cigarette while chatting up a girl who was sunbathing nearby (perhaps calling her attention to the features and benefits of said waterbed). Not having x-ray vision, he had no way of knowing that the hose had slipped out of the bed until water came pouring out the front door.

Incidents like these can strain the landlord-tenant relationship. But these cases are the exception; probably any issues your renters present will be mere bagatelles. At worst, it usually takes no more than three short months to get rid of a deadbeat tenant (but check with your local renter's rights council for the laws governing your community—you'll find them a friendly group).

We give you these stories to impress upon you that owning

and managing your own rental property can be a nightmare. The problems of possessing real estate, managing it, and dealing with its illiquidity can be solved by owning shares in REITs, but by all means, be a landlord if you prefer. Just be sure to keep a pager on your nightstand and a plumber's friend nearby for those crazy middle-of-the-night mishaps.

REITs SUBJECT THEMSELVES to the rigors of the stock market. However laughably inadequate the scrutiny of Wall Street analysts, the financial press, and corporate boards of directors of public companies like REITs may seem, they're like a brightly lit operating room compared with the smoke-filled backroom deals of the real-estate market outside their purview. REITs have a transparency and accountability previously unknown in real estate.

That said, we don't recommend that you buy REITs because of their transparency, nor for their liquidity, nor their powers of diversification, nor for the fact that you don't have to deal with tenants. It's also true that REITs have had quite a run up in the market over the past few years, but that's not why we recommend them, either. We recommend REITs for their yield—the income stream they generate. By law, a REIT must distribute 90 percent of its annual taxable income as dividends to its shareholders. These yields presently average about 4.6 percent.

Since this money was never taxed at the corporate level, these dividends are taxable as ordinary income. Except with the IRS, nothing is ever that simple.

REITs are required by law to pay dividends on their funds from operations, which add back the depreciation the properties suffer each year. For example, if you'd bought the Empire State Building in 1930, you could have depreciated it over the years, and by now it could be worth nothing for tax purposes, even though in reality, the building is worth a zillion dollars. Had it been in a REIT this whole time (however unlikely, since REITs didn't exist until 1960), this annual depreciation would have been returned to shareholders over the years. Usually, about 25 or 30 percent of the dividend yield from equity REITs constitutes such a return of capital and is ultimately taxed at the lower long-term capital-gains tax rate. This makes for a better after-tax yield on REITs, whose yields are pretty darn good anyway, as you'll soon see.

(By the way, we don't really care whether REITs' after-tax dividend yields are 50 basis points higher or lower than those from bonds or preferred stocks. Income investors will want to have as many sources of income as possible—that is, revenue sources that are diversified and likely to keep pace with the cost of living. It's not a contest; they just prefer to own them all, since diversification is one of the sweetest words in the English language as far as investors are concerned.)

Figure 9.1 compares the total risks and returns from owning REITs with those from stocks and bonds. REITs are very competitive, having similar total returns but with less monthly fluctuation in their prices. In this respect, the addition of REITs wonderfully diversifies a portfolio of stocks and bonds.

Figure 9.1: REITs vs. Stocks and Bonds 1978–2004

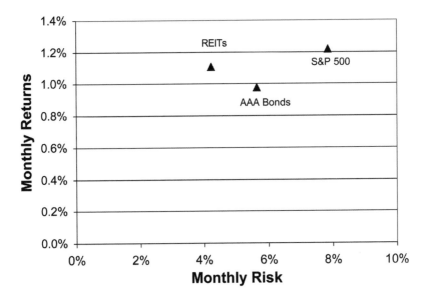

While it's often thought that tangible assets such as real estate provide a significant hedge against inflation, this is an oversimplification. Commercial real estate, like most other assets, is *negatively* correlated with inflation: When inflation is up, it will be down. This is because its income stream must be discounted back to the present at a higher rate of interest, which makes it worth less—not worthless, but worth less.

An inflationary environment may also stimulate overbuilding (the mortal enemy of the commercial real estate industry), which then leads to excess capacity and falling rents. Plus, inflation raises the interest rates on bonds, which mean that investors sell REITs until their returns more nearly are equilibrated with those of bonds and other interest-bearing instruments.

On the other hand, as noted, inflation significantly raises the value of the underlying properties in a REIT, which is factored into the share price, albeit as a less important factor than the yield.

How to Buy REITs

It's a simple matter for investors to participate in the entire REIT marketplace through ownership of a low-expense-index mutual fund that simply tracks the entire sector. There are a number to choose from listed in Table 9.1. There's no need to buy more than one, since they all basically sample from the same master list of 200 or so REITs, with slightly different weightings. Vanguard's is an open-end fund you can purchase from the company at the day's closing net asset value; the others are all exchange-traded funds that you buy and sell on the open market like stocks. This is the one-shot, easy approach to acquiring REIT income.

Table 9.1: REIT Index Funds 09/2004				
Fund	**Ticker**	**Index**	**Yield**	**Expense**
Vanguard REIT Index	VGSIX	Morgan Stanley REIT Index	4.8%	0.24%
Cohen & Steers Realty Majors	ICF	Cohen & Steers Realty Majors Index	4.5%	0.35%
Dow Jones Realty Index Fund	IYR	Dow Jones Realty Index	4.8%	0.60%
Wilshire REIT	RWR	Wilshire REIT Index	4.2%	0.26%

That said, we think a motivated income investor can do better. Let's take a closer look at how the world of REITs is divided. Table 9.2 shows the size of the various segments that make up the commercial real estate market.

Table 9.2 Equity REITs	
Segment	**Market Share**
Industrial/Office	31%
Shopping Centers	13%
Fashion Malls	13%
Retail Freestanding	2%
Apartments	18%
Manufactured Housing	1%
Diversified	6%
Hotel/Resort	4%
Health Care	4%
Self-Storage	4%
Specialty	4%

An index fund will typically own a "chocolate box" of assorted REITs weighted to approximate each segment's market share. *For the income-oriented investor, however, some of these market segments are more appealing than others.*

For example, the hotel/resort REIT business is highly correlated with the performance of the economy as a whole. In good times, there's a lot of business and vacation travel, so these properties perform well. But what about during bad times? People cut back on travel, and hotel rooms go unoccupied or are sold at drastic discounts. If you're counting on income from these hotels and resorts for food and clothing, you may be disappointed by your dividend checks.

Note that the leases underlying the rental of hotel rooms are 24 hours long. (By comparison, the leases for apartment buildings are typically one year, while commercial office and industrial spaces are often multiyear deals.) The same immediate sensitivity to the economy holds true for the fashion-mall segment. People love to shop and hang out at the fashion mall—it's a great way to kill a Saturday afternoon. But in a recession, many consumers hold off on buying that Ralph Lifschitz (now called "Lauren," for some reason) suit and make do with the outfits they have.

Next, consider the fashion mall's poor relation, the shopping center. You probably have one near your home. It has a grocery store as the anchor and is filled in with quotidian shops: a dry cleaners; a Starbucks; a drugstore; maybe a bank; and one of those stores where they sell scented candles, greeting cards, and gewgaws. Even in a severe economic downturn, people will still be buying milk and Pepto-Bismol and getting their clothes pressed. These stores make money in good times or bad (except maybe the knickknack store, but we've never understood those). They also pay their rents regardless of the economy.

To take extreme cases, Figure 9.2 shows the risks and rewards of investing in hotel/lodging REITs versus shopping center REITs from 1994 to 2003, courtesy of the National Association of Real Estate Investment Trusts (**www.nareit.com**). The shopping center REITs have a higher average monthly return and lower risk; the lodging REITs have lower returns and higher risks. To be fair, we should note that this period includes the horrible aftermath of 9/11, which gave the hotel business a black eye. Even so, as an income investor, you want to accentuate the shopping centers and de-emphasize the hotels in your portfolio.

Figure 9.2: REIT Sector Risks vs. Rewards 1994–2004

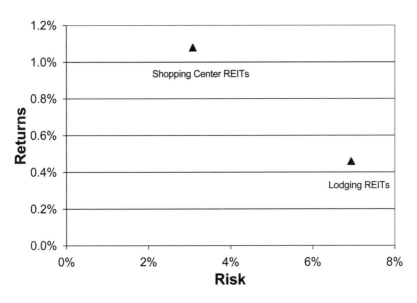

Income investors want to get a check on a regular basis. If there's a recession going on, you don't mind reading about it in the newspapers, and you'll be concerned, naturally—but in the end you want this to be the other guy's problem. You can try to avoid it by focusing your real-estate investments in market segments that are the most likely to be all-weather performers, trading the prospect of future growth for income today.

Once again, the mutual fund industry slumbers. There are no unleveraged REIT mutual funds specifically designed for income investors. This means that if you want one, you're going to have to create it yourself.

Your index-loving authors are loath to recommend individual stocks, but in this case we must. Our hope is that you can just buy these REITs and hold them forever, although it may be that something untoward happens between the time we write this and the time you want to go shopping. Remember our warning about the timeliness of stock "buy" lists, and use the same procedures that we proposed in Chapter 7 to double-check these REITs for steady and growing dividends.

We looked for REITs in segments that were noncyclical. We've already mentioned the shopping centers, and here are some others:

- **Manufactured Housing:** Please—don't calls us "trailer trash"! At present, some 22 million Americans live in ten million manufactured homes, accounting for 8 percent of the single-family housing stock in the United States. These homes are built off-site and brought to a parklike compound where they're mounted on cinder blocks and stay forever (or, possibly, until the next hurricane or tornado). The communities are cheerful and pleasant, with amenities such as swimming pools and putting greens. Residents own the homes (but lease the underlying land), turnover is low, and the checks to management are steady.

- **Health Care:** People get sick no matter how the economy is faring, and despite all the complaining about government regulation, doctors, emergency-care centers, and nursing-home operators still manage to pay their rents. An aging national demographic implies a steady demand for the full spectrum of health-care services.

- **Self-Storage Facilities:** Ever been inside one of these? Renting a 5' x 5' plot to store junk from your attic costs only slightly less than renting an apartment. These places make a shocking amount of money, and they're recession resistant, because when times are tough, people don't buy bigger homes—they move to smaller places and stow their extra gear instead.

This isn't to say that investing in these REIT segments will banish the boom-to-bust cycle endemic to real estate. But overweighting your real-estate portfolio in these market segments should give you a smoother ride and a regular paycheck.

We looked for companies that offered solid fundamentals and a ten-year track record of continual dividend increases. To be fair, we didn't want to discriminate against REITs from any market segments, so if they met our criteria, we included them. If we particularly fancied a REIT for some reason, we even bent the rule about a ten-year steadily rising, inflation-beating dividend a little, as long as its heart was in the right place. Here are our recommendations:

United Mobile Homes

Figure 9.3: United Mobile Homes Quarterly Dividends

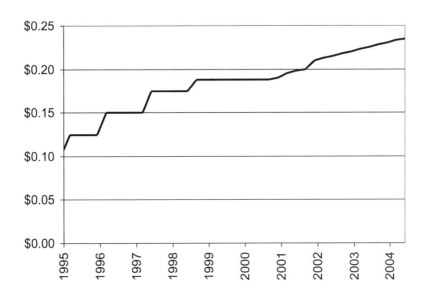

REIT:	United Mobile Homes
Website:	**www.umh.com**
Segment:	Manufactured housing
Market Cap:	113 MM
Current Price:	14.34
Dividend Yield:	6.5 percent
Ticker:	UMH

United Mobile Homes owns and operates a portfolio of 27 manufactured-home communities, including 6,300 sites in New Jersey, New York, Ohio, Pennsylvania, and Tennessee.

Public Storage

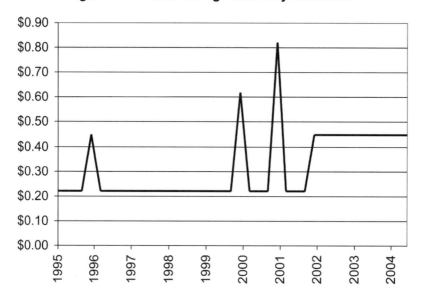

Figure 9.4: Public Storage Quarterly Dividends

REIT:	Public Storage
Website:	**www.publicstorage.com**
Segment:	Public storage
Market Cap:	4,692 MM
Current Price:	49.55
Dividend Yield:	3.6 percent
Ticker:	PSA

The largest player in the market, Public Storage manages over 800,000 self-service-storage spaces in 1,415 facilities in 80 U.S. and Canadian cities. It also offers storage-related services such as storage insurance, truck rentals, and the sale of supplies such as boxes and tape. In many markets, it offers local pickup as well as long-distance moving.

Kimco Realty

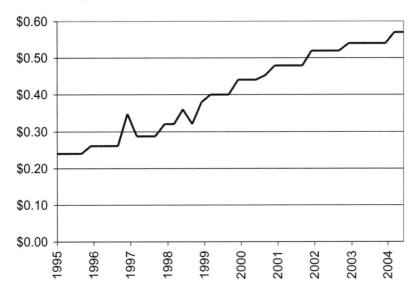

Figure 9.5: Kimco Realty Quarterly Dividends

REIT:	Kimco Realty
Website:	**www.kimcorealty.com**
Segment:	Shopping centers
Market Cap:	4,233 MM
Current Price:	51.30
Dividend Yield:	4.4 percent
Ticker:	KIM

Kimco Realty is the nation's largest publicly traded owner and operator of neighborhood and community shopping centers, with 700 properties in 43 states, Canada, and Mexico, comprising more than 100 million square feet of leasable space. These neighborhood shopping centers attract local-area customers through a supermarket, discount department store, or drugstore that anchors the property.

Regency Centers

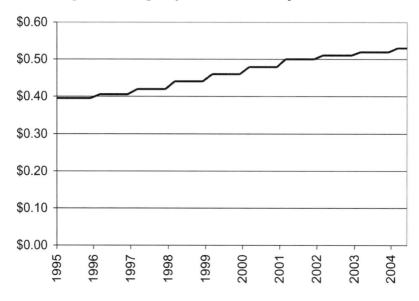

Figure 9.6: Regency Centers Quarterly Dividends

REIT:	Regency Centers
Website:	**www.regencyrealty.com**
Segment:	Shopping centers
Market Cap:	2,174 MM
Current Price:	46.49
Dividend Yield:	4.5 percent
Ticker:	REG

Regency Centers is a leading owner, operator, and developer of grocery-anchored neighborhood and community shopping centers. Regency has a $3.2 billion national real-estate portfolio that encompasses more than 262 high-quality-retail properties, primarily in the eastern United States. Spanning a total of nearly 30 million square feet, these properties are located in 46 metropolitan markets, including 18 of the largest 25 markets in the nation.

New Plan Excel Realty Trust

Figure 9.7: New Plan Excel Realty Trust Quarterly Dividends

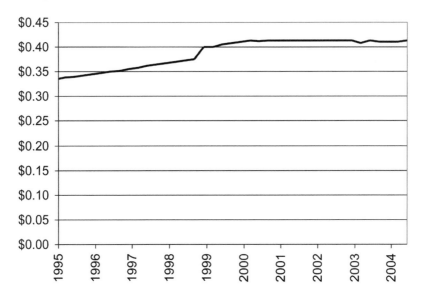

REIT:	New Plan Excel Realty Trust
Website:	**www.nprt.com**
Segment:	Shopping centers
Market Cap:	2,181 MM
Current Price:	25.00
Dividend Yield:	6.6 percent
Ticker:	NXL

New Plan Excel Realty Trust owns and manages community and neighborhood shopping centers, typically anchored by a Kmart or Wal-Mart and a grocery store. The REIT has a national portfolio of more than 400 properties located across 34 states and total assets of approximately $3.7 billion.

Realty Income

Figure 9.8: Realty Income Quarterly Dividends

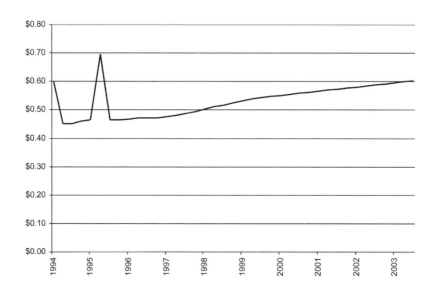

REIT:	Realty Income
Website:	**www.realtyincome.com**
Segment:	Freestanding retail
Market Cap:	1,513 MM
Current Price:	45.03
Dividend Yield:	5.4 percent
Ticker:	O

Realty Income owns 1,513 properties in 48 states, which it leases to freestanding national- and regional-chain restaurants, child-care centers, and automotive tire-and-lube centers. Sound boring? Unlike other REITs (which pay dividends quarterly), Realty Income pays dividends monthly—and they haven't missed a payment for 35 years. They've raised the dividend 31 times since becoming a public company in 1994.

Commercial Net Lease Realty

Figure 9.9: Commercial Net Lease Realty Quarterly Dividends

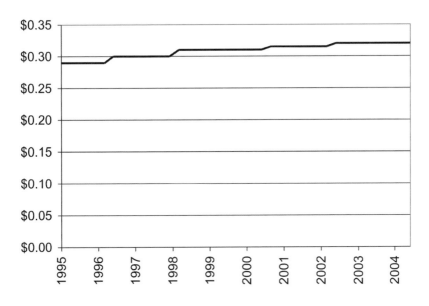

REIT:	Commercial Net Lease Realty
Website:	**www.cnlreit.com**
Segment:	Freestanding retail
Market Cap:	675 MM
Current Price:	18.22
Dividend Yield:	7.1 percent
Ticker:	NNN

Commercial Net Lease Realty and its subsidiaries own, build, and manage 279 single-tenant net-leased properties in the southern United States. Properties are leased to stores such as Wendy's, Best Buy, OfficeMax, and Pizza Hut. It has increased its dividend annually for the past 15 years, albeit by a small amount.

Health Care REIT

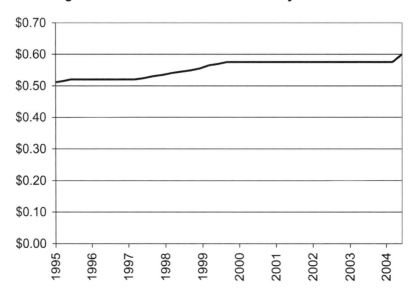

Figure 9.10: Health Care REIT Quarterly Dividends

REIT:	Health Care REIT
Website:	**www.hcreit.com**
Segment:	Health care
Market Cap:	1,216 MM
Current Price:	35.20
Dividend Yield:	6.7 percent
Ticker:	HCN

The nation's first health-care REIT, Health Care invests in 218 assisted-living facilities, 120 skilled-nursing facilities and eight specialty-care facilities located in 34 states and managed by 49 different operators for a total of $2.1 billion in net real-estate investments.

Universal Health Realty

Figure 9.11: Universal Health Realty Income Trust Quarterly Dividends

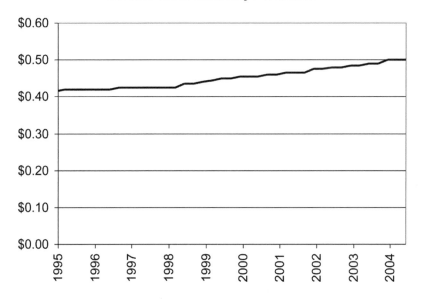

REIT:	Universal Health Realty
Website:	**www.uhrit.com**
Segment:	Health care
Market Cap:	313 MM
Current Price:	30.30
Dividend Yield:	6.6 percent
Ticker:	UHT

Universal Health Realty Income Trust specializes in health-care and human-service-related facilities. The trust has 44 investments located in 15 states, including acute-care hospitals, medical office buildings, rehabilitation hospitals, behavioral-health-care facilities, subacute-care facilities, surgery centers, and child-care centers.

Healthcare Realty Trust

Figure 9.12: Healthcare Realty Trust Quarterly Dividends

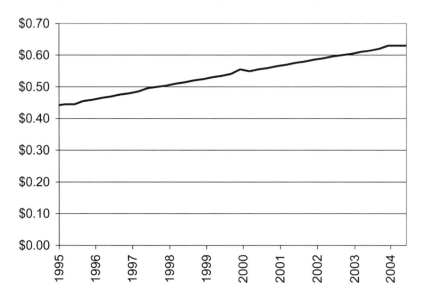

REIT:	Healthcare Realty Trust
Website:	**www.healthcarerealty.com**
Segment:	Health care
Market Cap:	1,360 MM
Current Price:	39.04
Dividend Yield:	6.5 percent
Ticker:	HR

Healthcare Realty Trust's portfolio is focused on outpatient services and medical offices located in 32 states, including contractual arrangements with 60 health systems. The company has investments of $1.8 billion in 237 real-estate properties, as well as mortgages totaling 12.7 million square feet. It also provides property-management services to more than 6.6 million square feet nationwide and has constructed medical-real-estate facilities valued at more than $500 million.

Archstone-Smith Trust

Figure 9.13: Archstone-Smith Trust Quarterly Dividends

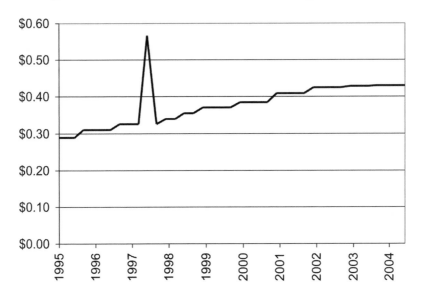

REIT:	Archstone-Smith Trust
Website:	**www.archstonecommunities.com**
Segment:	Apartments
Market Cap:	4,781 MM
Current Price:	31.64
Dividend Yield:	5.4 percent
Ticker:	ASN

Archstone-Smith Trust is a leading owner, developer, acquirer, and operator of apartments in major metropolitan areas across the country, with a total market capitalization of $9.6 billion. The company owns or has an ownership interest in 271 apartment communities comprising 93,878 units. The units are concentrated in eight major metropolitan areas, which account for 86 percent of net operating income. Two-thirds of the units are in garden communities under the Archstone Communities brand, while the rest are high-rise complexes under the Charles E. Smith brand.

BRE Properties

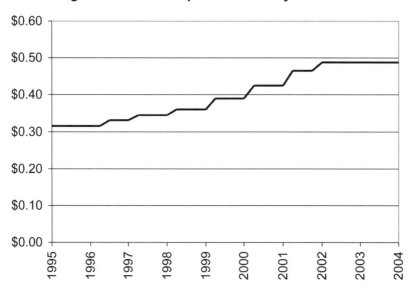

Figure 9.14: BRE Properties Quarterly Dividends

REIT:	BRE Properties
Website:	**www.breproperties.com**
Segment:	Apartments
Market Cap:	1,754 MM
Current Price:	38.35
Dividend Yield:	5.1 percent
Ticker:	BRE

BRE Properties acquires, develops, and manages apartment communities convenient to work, shopping, entertainment, and transportation in the supply-constrained western-U.S. markets. These include roughly 26,000 apartment units in some 85 residential communities.

Hospitality Properties Trust

Figure 9.15: Hospitality Properties Trust Quarterly Dividends

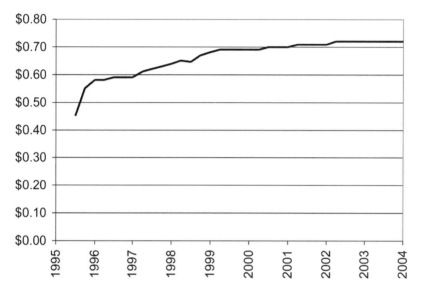

REIT:	Hospitality Properties Trust
Website:	**www.hptreit.com**
Segment:	Lodging
Market Cap:	2,554 MM
Current Price:	42.49
Dividend Yield:	6.8 percent
Ticker:	HPT

Hospitality Properties Trust buys, owns, and leases hotels. It currently owns 285 hotels with 38,489 hotel rooms in 10 major national brands. Leading chains include Courtyard Hotels (71 hotels), Residence Inns (37 hotels), Candlewood Suites (76 hotels), and Staybridge Suites (30 hotels).

Brandywine Realty Trust

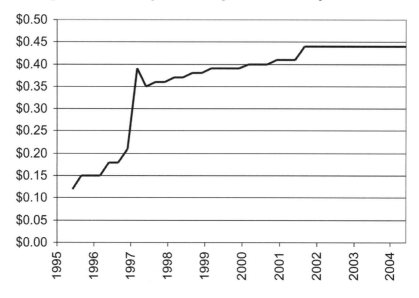

Figure 9.16: Brandywine Realty Trust Quarterly Dividends

REIT:	Brandywine Realty Trust
Website:	**www.brandywinerealty.com**
Segment:	Industrial and office space
Market Cap:	1,288 MM
Current Price:	28.48
Dividend Yield:	6.2 percent
Ticker:	BDN

Located in the Philadelphia area, Brandywine Realty is the largest REIT in the mid-Atlantic region, owning and operating some 25 industrial facilities and 200 office properties, according to Morningstar. They also own some 445 acres of undeveloped land.

Duke Realty

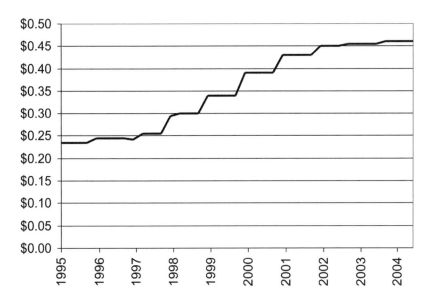

Figure 9.17: Duke Realty Quarterly Dividends

REIT:	Duke Realty
Website:	**www.dukerealty.com**
Segment:	Industrial and office space
Market Cap:	3,820 MM
Current Price:	33.20
Dividend Yield:	5.6 percent
Ticker:	DRE

Duke Realty provides leasing, property, and asset management and development services. It has more than 4,000 tenants occupying some 880 office, industrial, and retail properties comprising more than 109 million square feet. It also has 11 retail properties and 4,200 acres of undeveloped land.

Liberty Property Trust

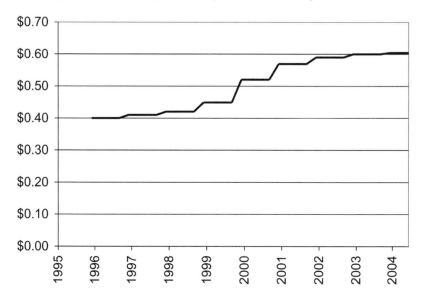

Figure 9.18: Liberty Property Trust Quarterly Dividends

REIT:	Liberty Properties Trust
Website:	**www.libertyproperty.com**
Segment:	Industrial and office space
Market Cap:	3,344 MM
Current Price:	39.84
Dividend Yield:	6.1 percent
Ticker:	LRY

Liberty Property Trust serves customers in the United States and United Kingdom through the acquisition, development, ownership, and management of office and industrial properties. One of the country's largest owners and managers of quality suburban-commercial real estate, Liberty's portfolio currently includes more than 650 properties in 16 markets. Concentrated in the mid-Atlantic, southeastern, and midwestern states, Liberty properties provide warehouse, distribution, manufacturing, research and development, and office facilities to more than 2,000 tenants in over 50 million square feet of space.

Mack-Cali Realty

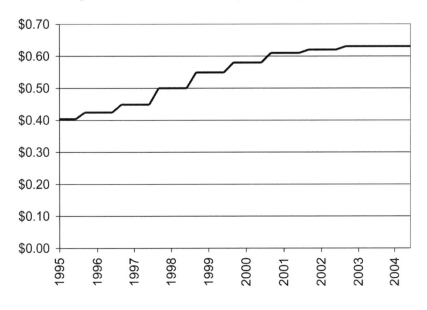

Figure 9.19: Mack-Cali Realty Quarterly Dividends

REIT: Mack-Cali Realty
Website: **www.mack-cali.com**
Segment: Office space
Market Cap: 2,051 MM
Current Price: 44.30
Dividend Yield: 5.7 percent
Ticker: CLI

Mack-Cali Realty Corporation owns and manages 260 buildings for approximately 30 million square feet of class "A" office and office/flex properties. Located primarily in the Northeast, Mack-Cali serves approximately 2,100 tenants. Mack-Cali's strategy is to focus on high-barrier-to-entry markets in the northeastern and mid-Atlantic regions.

Pennsylvania REIT

Figure 9.20: Pennsylvania REIT Quarterly Dividends

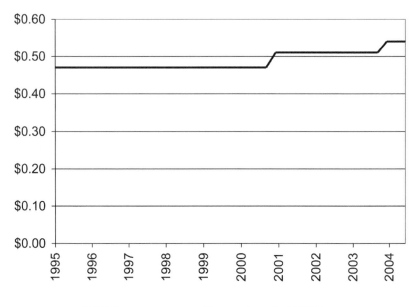

REIT:	Pennsylvania REIT
Website:	**www.preit.com**
Segment:	Diversified
Market Cap:	1,178 MM
Current Price:	38.66
Dividend Yield:	5.6 percent
Ticker:	PEI

Pennsylvania Real Estate Investment Trust, founded in 1960, has a primary investment focus on retail shopping malls and strip malls (approximately 33.6 million square feet) located in the eastern United States. Its portfolio currently consists of 50 properties in 14 states, and includes 4 multifamily-apartment properties that are held for sale, 14 shopping malls, 14 strip and power centers, and 4 industrial properties. It has paid dividends for 108 consecutive quarters.

Cousins Properties

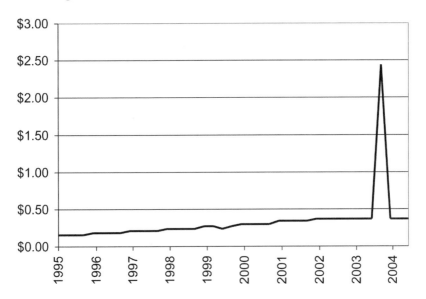

Figure 9.21: Cousins Properties Quarterly Dividends

REIT:	Cousins Properties
Website:	**www.cousinsproperties.com**
Segment:	Diversified
Market Cap:	1,514 MM
Current Price:	34.10
Dividend Yield:	4.4 percent
Ticker:	CUZ

Cousins Properties develops commercial-office, medical-office, and retail properties in selected markets throughout the United States—including office buildings, office parks, downtown mixed-use developments, regional malls, community shopping centers, and residential communities. The company's portfolio consists of interests in 12.6 million square feet of office and medical-office space, 3.1 million square feet of retail, and nearly 200 acres of strategically located land for future commercial development. As we go to press, Cousins has just announced a special $7.15 dividend for November 2004.

Lexington Properties Trust

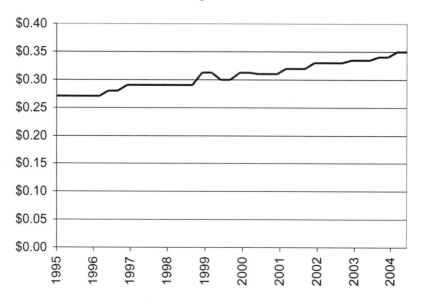

**Figure 9.22: Lexington Corporate Properties Trust
Quarterly Dividends**

REIT:	Lexington Properties Trust
Website:	**www.lxp.com**
Segment:	Diversified
Market Cap:	532 MM
Current Price:	21.70
Dividend Yield:	6.4 percent
Ticker:	LXP

Lexington Corporate Properties Trust is a real estate investment trust that invests in single-tenant net-lease properties throughout the United States. The company currently owns and/or manages 141 properties located in 34 states, totaling approximately 30 million square feet, including warehousing, distribution, and manufacturing facilities; office buildings; and retail properties.

As Table 9.3 shows, our high-dividend REIT portfolio still manages to offer you some diversification.

Table 9.3: The Stein/DeMuth REIT Steady Payers 09/2004			
Company	**Ticker**	**Yield**	**Sector**
United Mobile Homes	UMH	6.5%	Manufactured Housing
Public Storage	PSA	3.6%	Self-Storage
Kimco Realty	KIM	4.4%	Shopping Centers
Regency Realty	REG	4.5%	Shopping Centers
New Plan Excel	NXL	6.6%	Shopping Centers
Realty Income	O	5.4%	Freestanding
Commercial Net Lease Realty	NNN	7.1%	Freestanding
Health Care REIT	HCN	6.7%	Health Care
Unversal Health Realty	UHT	6.6%	Health Care
Healthcare Realty Trust	HR	6.5%	Health Care
Archstone-Smith Trust	ASN	5.4%	Apartment
BRE Properties	BRE	5.1%	Apartment
Hospitality Properties Trust	HPT	6.8%	Hotel
Brandywine Realty	BDN	6.2%	Industrial/Office
Duke Realty	DRE	5.6%	Industrial/Office
Liberty Property Trust	LRY	6.1%	Industrial/Office
Mack-Cali Realty	CLI	5.7%	Office
Pennsylvania REIT	PEI	5.6%	Diversified
Cousins Properties	CUZ	4.3%	Diversified
Lexington Properties Trust	LXP	6.4%	Diversified

Today, you can buy a portfolio of 100 shares of each of these REITs for about $71,000 and receive an annual yield of 5.6 percent that should keep up with inflation. Like any set of all-stars, some of these stocks will regress over time. However, the alternative—to select companies that pay inconsistent or poor dividends and hope they straighten out—doesn't seem like a particularly good strategy. The higher yield and lower risk that these REITs offer compared to the 4.6 percent return from the REIT indexes don't come free: They're a consolation prize for this group's lesser growth prospects. This is precisely the trade-off that the income investor is happy to make.

Looking back, their historical performance has actually been better than that of the REIT indexes, and as we'd hoped, showed less month-to-month fluctuation. Since we've selected REITs based on their historical dividend payments (screening out the weak sisters along the way), it isn't surprising that they beat the index. The index didn't know in advance who the winners would be, while we have the unfair advantage of hindsight.

Going forward, the performance of the two should converge, and the index certainly could do better on a total returns basis. Horses for courses: We're more concerned about providing you with a steady paycheck. Meanwhile, the lower risk of these higher-dividend payers is likely to be of enduring benefit. In spite of this hope, both the net asset value of this portfolio of REITs, as well as the Wilshire REIT index, dropped 15 percent during the panicked selling of April 2004. However, those prices rebounded quickly when it became apparent that interest rates weren't going through the roof as had been feared, and none of these REITs missed a dividend in that period.

Figure 9.23 shows the quarterly dividends these companies have been paying over the past decade. How sweet it must have been for shareholders to receive these inflation-beating checks quarter after quarter, each one usually a bit larger than the one before. How pleasant it must have been to drive to the bank to deposit them.

Figure 9.23: Stein-DeMuth REIT Quarterly Dividend Growth

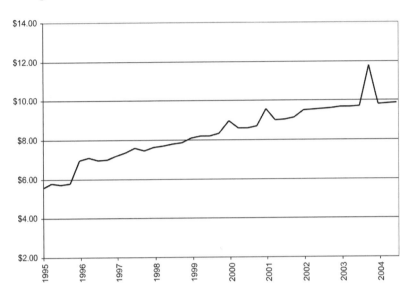

Table 9.4 shows a pared-down version of this REIT portfolio, the minimum REIT selection of individual stocks that we recommend holding. This would cost a little more than $30,000 to buy today and also yields a dividend of 5.6 percent. Since we're going to recommend later that REITs comprise 20 percent of your overall income allotment, this implies a total income portfolio value of $150,000 to get into choosing individual REIT securities.

If you have less than this to invest, just buy one of the excellent REIT index funds we mentioned earlier and leave it at that.

Table 9.4: The Stein/DeMuth REIT Minimum Portfolio 09/2004

Company	Ticker	Yield	Sector
United Mobile Homes	UMH	6.5%	Manufactured Housing
Kimco Realty	KIM	4.4%	Shopping Centers
Realty Income	O	5.4%	Freestanding
Healthcare Realty Trust	HR	6.5%	Health Care
Archstone-Smith Trust	ASN	5.4%	Apartment
Mack-Cali Realty	CLI	5.7%	Office
Hospitality Properties Trust	HPT	6.8%	Hotel
Cousins Properties	CUZ	4.3%	Diversified

Leveraged REIT Funds

Investors seeking a fatter yield than that afforded by the REIT indexes—or even that of our cherished REIT-dividend steady payers—have another option: buying a REIT mutual fund that's borrowed money to leverage the portfolio. You could do the same thing yourself by buying the REITs on margin in a brokerage account, but since the mutual fund is playing with millions of dollars (if not tens or hundreds of millions), they can borrow on vastly more advantageous terms than you can.

Table 9.5 shows what some of these funds are yielding right now. For comparison, remember that the REIT indexes presently yield 4.6 percent and our all-stars yield 5.6 percent; these leveraged REIT funds average 6.7 percent. (That's a head-to-head comparison, since all of them are taxed similarly.)

Table 9.5: Leveraged REIT Mutual Funds 09/2004			
Fund	**Ticker**	**Yield**	**Expense**
AEW Real Estate	RIF	6.8%	1.4%
AIM Select Real Estate Income	RRE	6.6%	1.0%
Cohen & Steers Advantage Income	RLF	7.2%	1.0%
Cohen & Steers Premium Income	RPF	6.7%	1.1%
Cohen & Steers Quality Income	RQI	6.8%	1.1%
Neuberger Berman Realty Income	NRL	6.3%	1.8%
Neuberger Berman Real Estate Income	NRI	6.4%	1.4%
Nuveen Real Estate Income	JRS	6.8%	2.1%
Real Estate Income Fund	RIT	7.0%	1.1%

Any one of these funds should suffice: They all hold a Monopoly board's worth of REIT securities and use leverage to boost the yield. Since these are closed-end funds, they typically sell at either a premium or a discount to the net-asset value of the securities they hold—and often at a discount at that. If you're going to buy one, it may be in your interest to select one that's at a deeper discount to NAV than others—especially where a single management company offers a number of essentially identical funds. Many of the investment organizations sponsoring them are currently (if temporarily) subsidizing a portion of these fees.

These funds were created in a low- and falling-interest-rate world to deliver the yield that investors craved. In the last few years, these leveraged REITs have been able to borrow at extraordinarily low rates and to reap amazing arbitrage between their rents and the price they pay for borrowed money, but this situation won't last forever.

They've all bought some time by purchasing swaps and other hedges against rapidly rising rates, but eventually their super-high yields should fall, at least somewhat. Plus, their leverage increases the month-to-month volatility, as they become plays on interest rates. As long as the rents the funds receive from the underlying properties are enough to service the loans and still leave money on the table for the managers to pay themselves and give investors a better return than they can get elsewhere, all should be well. If the spread between the loan service and the rents narrows, however, investors will wonder why they're taking on additional risk for so little extra return.

Consider carefully before making leveraged REIT funds the entirety of your real-estate-investment portfolio. You can't diversify away this risk by owning several of them: Since they're all concentrated in the same market sector, they'll rise or fall together. Investors proclaim their indifference to market shocks, but when you get a statement that shows you've lost 20 percent of your money in a single month (as happened to leveraged REIT funds during April 2004), your nerves will be tested.

In the first two weeks of that month alone, the Morgan Stanley REIT index tumbled 12 percent, wiping out two full years of dividend income via the loss of principal. The individual REITs in these funds are already leveraged (which is why their yields are so high to begin with), so owning REITs in a leveraged fund may be assuming more interest-rate risk than you'd really intended.

Figure 9.24 shows the difference in how rising interest rates affected a leveraged versus an unleveraged REIT fund during those unhappy 30 days.

Figure 9.24: Leveraged vs. Unleveraged REIT Funds April 2004

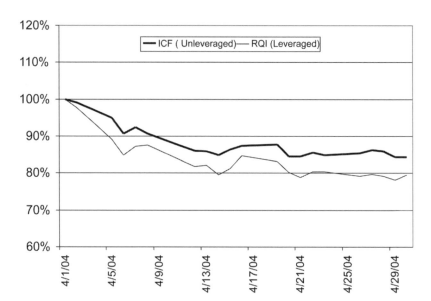

April 2004, though terrible, wasn't the end of the world. A month later, the unleveraged index fund in Figure 9.24 (ICF) was up 7.7 percent, and the leveraged fund (RQI) was up 7.5 percent. By October 2004, ICF was up 19 percent from the end of April, and RQI was up 17 percent. But this illustrates here (as elsewhere) the kinds of shocks to which income investors can be exposed. Meanwhile, the dividend checks kept on coming in while the values of the trusts fluctuated. This is a book about getting the most income you can for your investment dollar, and leveraged REITs are an important opportunity to do just that.

As significant as these securities are, we're going to switch our focus in the next chapter and take a look at another significant avenue of income: annuities.

CHAPTER TEN

The Special Case for Annuities

W̲e love annuities. They've saved the lives of people we know and love because they've provided that most rare and wonderful item: an insured lifetime of income, taking the anxiety and fear out of their lives as they entered retirement.

In the form of variable annuities, they made Ben Stein's parents beyond well-to-do and allowed them to enjoy extremely comfortable golden years. Partly because of what he saw in his own family, Ben is an honorary spokesperson for the National Retirement Planning Coalition, which is largely (but by no means entirely) backed by folks who sell variable annuities.

Buying an annuity is a decision with important financial consequences, and you have to make sure that it's the right one for you. The first thing you should know is that there are fundamentally two types of annuities: *fixed* and *variable*.

With a fixed annuity, an insurance company takes your payments and invests them in securities (usually bonds), where they grow for you tax-deferred. Then, at a date of your choosing, the insurance company starts paying your money back to you in fixed monthly installments that last until you die (or until your spouse dies, or some other predetermined date, which can even extend into your heirs' lifetimes).

With a variable annuity, the insurance company takes your money and invests it in the stock or bond markets or both, where it grows tax-deferred. Then, as of a given date, you're paid back a monthly amount that is either fixed or, if you so choose, can vary with the fortunes of the underlying equity or bond investments. Variable annuities often have a death benefit, such that your estate receives any money left in the account. There are also ones that protect the owner against stock market downturns. The specific provisions will differ considerably from policy to policy.

Obviously, certain contingencies determine how much the insurance company will agree to pay each month, such as actuarial tables that predict how long the annuity holders will live and data on interest rates that tell the insurer what it can afford to pay. When you buy a lifetime fixed annuity, you're betting against the actuarial tables that you'll live longer than the average annuity buyer of your age and sex—and, yes, insurance companies have figured out that only healthy people buy annuities.

Annuities can also be either immediate or deferred. With an immediate annuity, you give the insurance company a pile of cash to buy the annuity, and their payments back to you begin, well, immediately.

With a deferred annuity, on the other hand, you make a single payment or regular payments over time to the insurance company toward that future date when your accumulated contributions will be annuitized and the distributions back to you will commence. The insurer invests your money in stocks, bonds, or anything else within a small ambit that allows the cash to accumulate and then starts paying you at a later date. Since Americans are notorious spendthrifts, this form of enforced savings for retirement can be highly salutary.

In the past, annuities got a bad rap from high-pressure commissioned salespeople who preyed on the fears of senior citizens to sell them annuities, regardless of whether they really were appropriate investments for those individuals. In addition, fees could be high and inscrutable. This is a shame, because annuities play an extremely important role in personal finance. The careful shopper can, without question, find ones whose fees are reasonable.

When much of corporate America found that providing defined-benefit pension plans was too expensive, they kicked workers into 401(k)s. The upshot was that every worker had to plan for a retirement where he or she might live to be 100, even though only a small percentage would actually require support this long.

Think about the implications: If you have to plan to stretch your pot of money until you reach 100, even though you might only live to age 80, the monthly paycheck from your nest egg has to shrink dramatically to cover this low-probability contingency, eating away at your standard of living in the process.

Here the annuity comes to your rescue. When you purchase an annuity, you rejoin the retirement pool. The annuity sponsor can distribute the risk rationally, planning for most people to live average life spans, instead of everyone being centenarians. This allows investors in aggregate to receive more money during their lifetimes, as those who unfortunately die early on the bell-shaped longevity curve will effectively pay for those long-lived ones at the other end.

Many (if not most) baby boomers are going to reach retirement with grossly inadequate savings. By purchasing immediate annuities upon retirement with what savings they do have, they'll be able to convert their nest eggs into the highest possible income stream to support them through their remaining years. This is because the annuity pays back not only interest but also principal. This is an actuarial calculation, not a free gift.

These advantages make annuities extremely important for this generation (of which your authors are charter members). But they still have to be approached sensibly, so we offer you these tips:

- Give high-pressure salespeople and those who refuse to show you the full range of their products the brush-off, politely but firmly.

- Annuities come with more features than a Swiss Army knife and are so complicated that even most financial advisors don't understand them. The interest rate or monthly payment, for example, is only one piece of the puzzle. Don't sign anything unless the provisions are crystal clear to you—and to the person selling it. Don't be afraid to admit that you don't understand this or that provision.

- You know how they always say to read the prospectus? When it comes to annuities, you'd better *really* read the prospectus. Don't be placated by the blandishments of your broker or insurance rep. To borrow a saying from show business, "If it's not on the page, it's not on the stage."

- Unbiased advice about annuities is hard to come by. A broker or agent may be eager to sell one in order to get a commission, while an investment advisor may steer you away from this option because he or she doesn't want to lose that portion of the assets under management. Be sure you know what's in it for them, either way.

- Shop around. This is a big step. Do it carefully.

- The decision to annuitize your savings is often irrevocable, and even when possible, high surrender charges can make changing your mind later a costly mistake. You can find annuities with lower surrender charges or none at all, and with more flexibility than you might have thought possible. A careful shopper will be well rewarded here.

- A fixed annuity is an enormous bet on interest rates (that they won't go up) and takes on tremendous purchasing-power risk. If severe inflation hits, a fixed annuity will be a problem. *Don't put all your money into a single fixed annuity.* Dollar-cost average into several fixed annuities over a series of years in order to diversify interest-rate risk, or buy them when long-term interest rates are high. If interest rates are already high, they have more chance of coming down than going higher. Plus, there are certain annuities that will sell you inflation protection, so look for—and at—them carefully. They may well be your best bets.

- When you buy a fixed annuity, you're making a whopping bet on the financial integrity of the sponsoring company. If they go out of business, there may not be any money to pay you, no matter what the contract says. It makes sense to go with a highly rated, long-lived, large company that is, as they say, too big to fail.

- *The Wall Street Journal's* Jonathan Clements has pointed out that postponing the purchase of an immediate fixed annuity to as late a point as possible in life can usefully overcome a low-interest-rate environment by compressing the return of principal into a shorter period of time—your projected remaining life span.

- Since annuities typically consume your entire principal along the way, once again they offer a higher distribution yield than other investments that don't hand you back your principal in this fashion. While the return of principal isn't taxed, all the rest that you receive is ordinary income (that is, it's taxed at your marginal rates, not at Bush's 15 percent, as dividends and long-term capital gains presently are).

- Tax-wise, the best assets to store inside a deferred variable annuity are those that throw off lots of ordinary taxable income along the way, such as real estate investment trusts or bonds (we are indebted to the neurons of William Bernstein for this *aperçu*). This allows you to take full advantage of the tax-deferred properties of these investments.

- Buying an immediate variable annuity inside a tax-deferred plan such as a 401(k) or Keogh upon retirement makes the most sense, since withdrawals from these plans are taxed at ordinary-income rates in any event.

- A variable annuity is often, but not always, a bet on the performance of the stock market. As we demonstrated like a Euclidean theorem in *Yes, You Can Time the Market!*, some times are far better than others for buying stocks. Is now one of them? Go to **www.stein-demuth.com** for updates.

- Take a close look at index annuities, which allow you to lock in gains somewhere between those of the stock and bond markets, while protecting you against the loss of principal.

We admit that we're biased about annuities because, again, one of our sets of parents invested in variable annuities and made fantastic returns. Solid arguments can be made for putting a sizable portion of an investment pool leading up to retirement in variable annuities (once your other tax-deferred options are funded), and/or a sizable chunk of post-retirement income in immediate annuities. But talk to your financial planner about these investments and shop around. They aren't all the same, and some are far better than others. But variable annuities, carefully purchased and fully understood, can be an astonishing and even indispensable gift to the investor. Investigate fully, and consider them seriously for your retirement plan. If you choose wisely, you will be delighted by the results.

Now we turn to some investments that may be riskier than those we've examined up to this point. Fasten your seat belts.

CHAPTER ELEVEN

Approach These Income Strategies with Caution

Having been around the block a couple times, down 40 miles of bad road, and bitten more than once where our investments are concerned, your authors have come to be circumspect about a number of income strategies. The markets, which have tossed us back and forth between the pitchforks of greed and fear, have been great teachers of humility. If making money were easy, after all, everyone would be rich. Wall Street is in the business of creating financial service products to sell. While they (the sellers) enrich themselves in the process, we (the buyers) are not always so fortunate. Given this fact, what follows are a few investment ideas that we think it pays to approach with some skepticism.

Mortgage REITs

Don't be fooled by the name: A mortgage REIT doesn't own or manage real estate at all. It's a purely financial entity that borrows money (borrows short) and invests it in pools of mortgages (lends long). It operates inside the legal structure of a REIT, so 90 percent of the profits must be distributed every year, and its dividends are taxable as ordinary income.

You might think that with mortgage rates already rebounding from their historic lows, all the money possible has been made in the mortgage business. Not so. These REITs don't care what mortgage rates are; they only care about the *spread* between their borrowing costs and their lending income. In other words, as long as short-term rates are lower than long-term rates, these companies (which are substantially leveraged) can make money; when the yield curve is flat or inverted, they won't.

Unlike the REITs we've touted before, these aren't all-weather investments. In bad economic times, or if the real estate bubble bursts, people may default on their loan payments. However, not all mortgage REITs invest in residential mortgages: Some may favor commercial-property mortgages, construction loans, or subprime/high-yield loans, each of which has different risk characteristics.

You also have to consider the amount of leverage each mortgage REIT uses, which varies from company to company. Since management bases its fee on the size of its asset pool, there's an ever-present temptation to err on the side of using too much leverage. These factors make mortgage REITs difficult to analyze and value.

The dividends these investments pay aren't going to be consistent and rise little by little, as with the equity REITs we favored earlier. If you buy a mortgage REIT, you're in for Mr. Toad's wild ride. Yields have been quite generous (9 percent or more) in recent years. They definitely have their plus side, but again, caution is advised.

Here are two of these opportunities that we like better than others, at least for the moment. Your list may vary.

Annaly Mortgage Management

Figure 11.1: Annaly Mortgage Management Quarterly Dividends

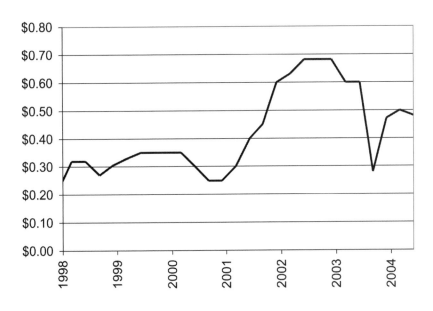

REIT:	Annaly Mortgage Management
Website:	**www.annaly.com**
Sector:	Mortgage REIT
Market Cap:	1,576 MM
Current Price:	17.13
Dividend Yield:	13.0 percent
Ticker:	NLY

Annaly Mortgage Management purchases mortgage-backed securities, which are ownership interests in mortgage loans made by savings and loans, commercial banks, and mortgage bankers. All of Annaly's securities are classified as "available for sale," recorded at market value (determined by the average price provided by three independent sources), and announced quarterly. The assets in the portfolio are Fannie Mae, Ginnie Mae, or Freddie Mac agency securities, which carry actual or implied AAA ratings. There are no derivatives, interest-rate swaps, currency swaps, or total-return swaps in the portfolio. All of Annaly's assets are issued by government agencies and carry the implied or actual AAA rating that comes with that backing. In addition, Annaly structures its portfolio with a combination of adjustable-, floating-, and fixed-rate mortgage-backed securities so that it can weather a variety of different interest-rate environments.

RAIT Investment Trust

Figure 11.2: RAIT Investment Trust Quarterly Dividends

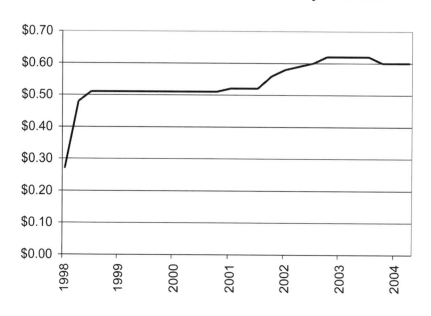

REIT:	RAIT Investment Trust
Website:	**www.raitinvestmentrust.com**
Sector:	Mortgage REIT
Market Cap:	490 MM
Current Price:	27.35
Dividend Yield:	8.8 percent
Ticker:	RAS

RAIT Investment Trust is a specialty finance company focused on the midsized commercial real estate industry, primarily in the Northeast. RAIT creates tailored financial solutions for its borrowers, and it provides structured financing to private and corporate owners of real estate. RAIT offers senior mortgage debt as well as subordinated financing, such as mezzanine, bridge, and conduit loans. RAIT also acquires real estate for its own account.

YOU MIGHT WANT TO CONSIDER adding a mortgage REIT to your real-estate portfolio, if and when the underlying economic conditions warrant—or you might not. Just don't count on it for the grocery money. The dividends are spectacular, but the risk is sizable.

A slightly more conservative option would be to buy a leveraged closed-end mortgage bond fund. Here you're betting that the borrowing costs will stay below the (floating) mortgage rates. Table 11.1 shows a couple that we like better than others.

Table 11.1: Leveraged Mortgage Bond Funds 09/2004					
Fund	**Ticker**	**Yield**	**Maturity**	**Credit**	**Expense**
BlackRock Income Trust	BKT	8.7%	4.2 yrs	AAA	1.4%
Pimco Commercial Mort.	PCM	9.0%	5.0 yrs	BBB	1.5%

Junk Bonds

One of your humble authors (Ben Stein) was a major player in exposing the junk-bond scandals of the 1980s. The popular illusion at the time was that high-yield bonds were the perfect investment—that is, while owning a single high-yield bond might be risky, owning a basket of them diversified away all risk. After all, the loss rate due to default was supposed to be so low that it was easily offset by the high interest payments from these bonds. Some experts also believed that the preference of banks and insurance companies for high-credit-quality bonds led the market to anomalously underprice low-credit-quality bonds.

Drexel Burnham Lambert took advantage of this impression and started passing out high-yield bonds like Junior Mints, and pretty soon everyone got into the act. The world became awash in a sea of junk paper, and when the loss rate proved to be far higher than anticipated—largely because of fraud in the issuance and accounting for junk and the creation of junk-holding financial pyramid schemes, which vanished in the late '80s and early '90s—much of it went down the drain.

Fifty-five federally insured, Drexel-controlled, junk-holding savings and loans went bankrupt, as did dozens of large insurance companies. Plenty of workers lost their jobs as companies were bought out and looted, pension plans went bust, and insurers lost their investment pools.

And the buyers of junk bonds and junk bond mutual funds? They lost a supertanker full of money. It's true that after those events there was a substantial rally in the junk that survived, but the bonds that were dead offered only modest recoveries in default.

Junk bonds have their uses, but they also have substantial risks. The hazards are definitely lower now that junk isn't part of an ongoing scam as it was under Drexel, though.

Figure 11.3 shows how steeply yields decline and risk increases once you slide off the investment-grade-bond credit scale. The data are from the Lehman Brothers High Yield indexes, 1986 to 1998. Since the index uses "trader" pricing and simply drops those bonds that default after a certain point (rather than subtracting them from the total returns of the index), these numbers considerably overstate the returns and underweight the risks of junk-bond investing.

Figure 11.3: Junk Bond Risks & Returns 1986–1998

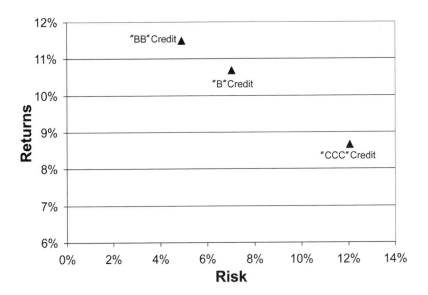

The moral: Invest in junk bonds at your peril. If you decide to plunge in, at least protect yourself in these ways:

1. Limit them to a bite-sized portion of your holdings.

2. Only join the party when their yield spread above Treasury bonds is wide (five percentage points or more).

3. Invest only in the least junky credit end of the junk-bond spectrum.

To see an example of the impact of the credit spread on junk-bond yields, look at Table 11.2.

Table 11.2: Two High-Yield Funds 2003			
Fund	**% BB or Better**	**Yield**	**Ann. 3-Yr. Returns**
BB-Rated Fund	72%	7.3%	6.20%
B-Rated Fund	31%	7.3%	0.31%

The BB-rated junk-bond fund has the better credit quality, with 72 percent of its portfolio in at least BB-rated bonds. Surprisingly, both funds offered the same yield during 2003: a handsome 7.3 percent. But look at the difference in the total returns these funds delivered over the past three years. The low-credit-quality "junk" fund, due to defaults, offered investors a terrible annualized 0.31 percent return.

Table 11.3 is a short list of funds to consider if you're determined to forge ahead with junk bonds. The Columbia fund is closed to new investors as of this writing, although at some point they'll reopen their doors—probably at the exact moment when you won't want to buy it.

Table 11.3: BB-Rated Bond Funds 09/2004				
Fund	**Ticker**	**Yield**	**Maturity**	**Expense**
Columbia High Yield Z	CMHYX	6.4%	4.4 yrs	0.82%
Neuberger Berman High Inc.	NBHIX	6.2%	5.9 yrs	0.90%
Vanguard High Yield	VWEHX	7.4%	6.7 yrs	0.23%

Loan-Participation Funds

A much safer subset of junk bonds consists of what are called *loan-participation funds* or *senior-income funds*. This latter cognomen is not intended to denote that these are good sources of income for senior citizens, but only means that their debt is "senior" to other monies the company owes, meaning that it will be repaid first.

These loan-participation funds buy short-term, low-credit-quality debt as portions of a larger debt instrument at a floating rate, usually tied to some short-term interest rate index. Most of the debt is below investment-grade-credit quality. These funds (shown in Table 11.4) shine during an economic recovery when their floating interest rates are rising and their companies' credit quality is improving, but will suffer inordinately during an economic decline when interest rates and credit quality are declining.

The Fidelity offering is an open-end opportunity, while the closed-end funds all use leverage, making for double-barreled thrills.

Table 11.4: Loan Participation Funds 09/2004			
Fund	**Ticker**	**Yield**	**Expense**
OPEN-END			
Fidelity Floating Rate High Income	FFRHX	3.1%	0.9%
CLOSED-END			
Eaton Vance Senior Income Trust	EVF	5.8%	2.7%
ING Prime Rate Trust	PPR	5.7%	2.4%
Nuveen Senior Income	NSL	5.6%	1.6%
Pimco Floating Rate Income	PFL	4.5%	1.2%
Van Kampen Senior Income	VVR	4.6%	2.2%

Income-Deposit Securities

Wall Street's cauldron has recently bubbled up a new junk product called *income deposit securities,* or *IDS* for short. These pay astronomic yields for the simple reason that the underlying companies can't raise money in any other way. But one provision that's raising eyebrows is that management can suspend payments for up to two years before bondholders have the right to force them into bankruptcy (as opposed to 30 days for most traditional bonds). Another drawback is that their tax status is as yet undetermined.

These securities would be good buys for anyone who believes that every story has a happy ending. In an economic downturn or a rising-interest-rate environment, the sky could fall.

Convertible Securities

A convertible bond allows the holder to exchange it for a share (or many shares) of a company's stock if the stock reaches a predetermined price. When the stock sells below this level, the bond trades and fluctuates in price like any other bond. When the stock exceeds the prespecified point, then the bond trades in price like the stock. It might be thought of as a bond that has potential for capital appreciation like a stock.

Usually (although by no means always), companies with lower credit quality offer convertible securities as a carrot to induce people to lend them money at a lower interest rate than would otherwise be demanded, so all the usual warnings about low credit quality apply. This embedded opportunity for capital appreciation doesn't come free; it means that the convertible bond pays a lower coupon as compensation. For this reason, we think that investors looking for the highest income per unit of risk should look elsewhere. By using leverage, convertible-income funds can offer a high yield, but then, so would leveraging Aunt Tillie.

Nuveen has come up with an interesting use for convertible bonds in their closed-end Preferred and Convertible Income Funds (tickers: JPC, JQC), which hold a combination of preferred stock and convertible bonds. They're long-term, investment-grade, leveraged funds that pay a yield of 8.3 percent as of September 2004.

What's intriguing is that Nuveen is using preferreds and convertibles in combination to hedge the portfolio. If interest rates fall, the preferred stocks should become more valuable due to their high yields. If rates rise, the preferreds fall in value, but the convertibles should increase with improving economic conditions (since below their strike price, convertibles tend to trade like stocks). One hand washes the other, and both wash the face. In any case, that's the theory.

Reverse Mortgages

Most Americans' single biggest asset is their home. If you've been dutifully making house payments to the mortgage company for the past 30 years, it's only natural to wonder if it isn't about time they returned the favor and started making payments back to you. The financial-services industry got to wondering about this, too, and pretty soon a clamshell floated up to the shore and, like Venus, out stepped the reverse mortgage. The decision to get one may be the last major financial decision you'll ever make.

(Over the years we've noticed that many of these "reverse" ideas don't pan out as well as expected. The reverse play in football is a perfect example. And what about reverse psychology, reverse discrimination, and reverse osmosis? The reverse mortgage idea seems unlikely to reverse this trend.)

The reverse mortgage is a home-equity loan that you can take either in a lump sum or as a monthly cash installment. Best of all, you generally don't have to pay it back until you die (at which point it's not really your problem anymore, is it?), or until you move (when you can use the cash from the sale of the house). Unlike in the case of an ordinary mortgage or home-equity line, no monthly repayments are required, so you don't need to document any source of income to qualify. You only have to be at least 62 years old and, most important, to own your home.

Our concern isn't with the first generation of reverse mortgages, which were outright scams that have been put out of business. We're concerned about the second generation of reverse mortgages that are scams that have *not* been put out of business.

Consider these warning signs:

- Reverse-mortgage "counseling" is provided by the same people who lend you the money. This is like getting car-purchase "counseling" from the guy trying to sell you a Bentley. Actually, it's worse, because reverse mortgages are bewilderingly complicated.

- Loan fees are significantly higher than those for regular mortgages.

- Fees are paid up-front, and they start compounding from day one, while the loan is usually dribbled out over time. Fees eat away substantial amounts of home value before you receive the first dime.

- Interest rates charged are three to five percentage points higher than for 30-year mortgage loans.

- Speaking of fees, in addition to a 2 percent "origination" fee, there can be points, mortgage-insurance premiums, and closing costs for title search, appraisals, surveys, credit checks, taxes, and loan-recording fees.

- You also get to pay a monthly "servicing" fee of $30. Sound like peanuts? Try compounding it over 20 years.

- Sometimes you get to pay the bank a "maturity" fee—a percentage of your home's sale price at the termination of the reverse mortgage.

- There can also be a "shared-appreciation" fee based on the increase in your home's value during the life of the loan. Despite its "I'm okay, you're okay" name, which sounds like you're going to get a group hug, this fee can end up being larger than the entire amount of the loan.

- Once you move out for whatever reason, the bank can force you to sell and pay them back. What if the neighborhood changes? What if you require long-term care?

For some people, though, a reverse mortgage may be the only answer. The AARP has a pamphlet called "Home Made Money" on their Website **(www.aarp.org)** that can help you sort out the pitfalls.

Long-Term Bonds

The rewards from owning long-term bonds are overshadowed by their much higher risks (defined here as "standard deviation," the month-to-month fluctuation of the price around the average).

Figure 11.4 shows some of the risks and rewards available from Treasury-bond funds over the past few years.

Figure 11.4: Treasury Bond Risks vs. Returns 2000–2003

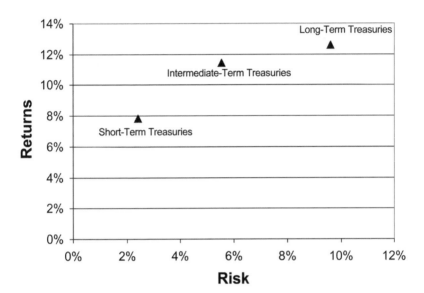

While you rack up a big gain in yield by moving out from short-term to intermediate-term bonds (along with a sizable helping of risk—by which we mean volatility in the price of the bonds or funds), you gain less than one percentage point in yield for taking on four more percentage points of added risk by moving from intermediate-term to the long bond. Nor does the situation change if you substitute long-term corporate bonds (see Figure 11.5).

Figure 11.5: Corporate Bond Risks vs. Returns 2000–2003

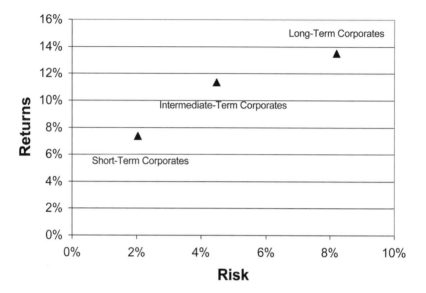

You gain roughly equal measures of risk and reward by moving from short- to intermediate-term corporate bonds, but twice the risk per unit of return for going longer than this.

How much you risk and how much you gain from moving out to longer-maturity bonds is a function of the shape of the yield curve (which we showed in Figure 3.1 on p. 15) that applies over the period you're invested, and that shape is constantly changing. At some times, the spread in yields between the intermediate-term and the long-term maturity bonds might be great enough to turn your heads. We don't say that this will happen very often, or that even when it does that you should bet the farm. We merely want to point out that there may be a time when going long will offer a reasonable premium in yield to the income investor. Our lust to go long is generally satisfied by going intermediate-term, though.

Royalty Trusts and Master Limited Partnerships

A royalty trust is a financial wrapper for holding a group of assets and their operating companies. Despite their regal sound, they have nothing to do with Prince Charles or members of any other royal family. These trusts own hard assets such as oil reserves, timber, natural gas, or minerals. The cash flows generated by the sale of the trusts' assets are passed directly through to the shareholder.

Royalty trusts aren't partnerships, and all units within them are created equal. With a master limited partnership (MLP), however, there's a master partner who owns a 2 percent stake and receives an incentivized dividend distribution, and then there are rest of the investors who own common limited partnership units. Should managers display excessive self-interest (as they've been known to do), this structure allows them to operate the companies to enrich themselves at the expense of the limited partners who underwrite them. Back in the 1980s, MLPs were often little more than tax-shelter scams, and they have yet to fully recover from that well-deserved bad publicity.

Another difference between these two options has to do with the fact that royalty trusts tend to be concerned with energy exploration, while the MLPs tend to focus on oil and gas processing and distribution. In practice, this makes the income from royalty trusts less susceptible to interest-rate risk, as inflation represents a large component of that danger, and the underlying oil and gas resources the trusts own act as a hedge. A trade-off is that the income from royalty trusts will fluctuate with commodity prices—a thrill ride—while presumably the income from just storing, refining, and piping the energy in the MLP is more stable.

The yields from these trusts and partnerships presently range up to about 15 percent. Since risk and reward go hand in hand for investors, this should be enough to make you raise an eyebrow. Let's consider some of the risks.

Royalty trusts aren't bottomless cornucopias of natural resources. After all, oil wells run dry; you don't see the forest for the trees are eventually cut down; and as natural gas is sold today, less remains to sell tomorrow. This means that every dividend check you receive effectively includes a return of principal, since the underlying assets are being depleted.

This cash being passed back to you enlarges the apparent yield. Unlike with a bond, there's no return of principal at maturity—

there's only what you can sell your trust shares for in the marketplace. And if the underlying resource is gone, those shares may not sell for much. In that respect, these trusts are more like an annuity, where your principal is parceled back to you over the life of the investment—although unlike an annuity, the payout can be anything but consistent or lifelong.

The amount that's a return of capital varies from company to company. Most of these trusts have a reserve of about ten years' worth of raw materials, so in order to stay in operation, the trustees need to plow money back into acquiring new resources. Replenishing these reserves can be expensive, and raising this investment capital from the market to buy them necessarily impacts the existing shares—namely, yours. You might buy into what looks like a torrent of dividends today only to discover that management has used your money to buy expensive new forestry land, and that the dividend going forward won't be so lavish.

Being commodity-based, the price of royalty trusts will fluctuate with the value of the underlying assets. As the price of oil and natural gas has soared with geopolitical events over the past few years, so has the underlying value of the oil wells and natural-gas deposits that these trusts hold. That makes them look especially good right now—but this outcome was by no means inevitable.

Many of these royalty trusts are located in Canada, a country that is the Pamela Anderson of natural resources (that is, well endowed), which adds the spice of currency risk to the equation. If the Canadian dollar appreciates against the U.S. dollar, investors will be happy, while if the Canadian dollar falls, tears will flow.

The Canadian trusts receive a tax break: Their dividend distributions are taxed at the maximum 15 percent tariff under the Bush tax plan. They're also subject to a 15 percent withholding tax in Canada, but U.S. investors can recoup this on their federal taxes—if they don't mind throwing some extra money at their accountants to retrieve it. In some cases, the companies get special exploration and depreciation allowances that can be passed along to taxpayers as well.

Table 11.5 lists a few of these trusts and their yields, just to get your pulses racing.

Table 11.5: Royalty Trusts 09/2004			
Trust	**Ticker**	**Business**	**Yield**
BP Prudhoe Royalty Trust	BPT	Oil & Gas	8.0%
Dominion Resources	DOM	Gas	8.2%
Great Nothern Iron	GNI	Iron	6.4%
Mesabi Trust	MSB	Iron	7.0%
Permian Basin Royalty Trust	PBT	Oil & Gas	7.1%

As exciting as these are, you still have to ask the question: Why would the owners and operators of these companies put their assets into a trust in the first place? This wasn't a charitable gesture; they did it to make money. They believed that investors would pay a higher price for their assets than they could obtain from a competitor (who might bring a great deal of expertise into pricing the underlying assets) or than they could get just by hanging on to them and operating the business themselves.

This, plus (a) the currency risk, (b) the difficulty of pricing these securities accurately, and (c) the wild card of commodity prices, makes us leery of advising you to put more than a teaspoon of sugar into these beguiling assets.

Master limited partnerships in oil and gas transmission are even more sensitive to interest-rate risk. Unlike the self-depleting natural resources behind royalty trusts, the pipeline is a durable piece of technology unlikely to become obsolete soon. But the fact that the limited partners take the risks while management gets a free ride makes us uncomfortable. If you put a gun to our heads, we might mention the MLPs in Table 11.6. Put only as much money into them as you'd take to Las Vegas for the weekend.

Table 11.6 Master Limited Partnerships 09/2004			
Trust	**Ticker**	**Business**	**Yield**
Buckeye Partners	BPL	Pipelines	5.9%
Cedar Fair	FUN	Amusement Parks	5.9%
Kinder Morgan Energy	KMP	Pipelines	5.9%
MarkWest Energy Partners	MWE	Processing	6.2%
W.P. Carey & Co.	WPC	Real Estate	5.9%

Oh, and one more thing: When you buy a royalty trust or master limited partnership, you don't get the standard Form 1099 detailing your dividend income at the end of the year, as you do for your ordinary stocks and mutual funds. Instead, you get something called a K-1 partnership distribution form. This means that tax filing is going to become more complicated (and more expensive). The silver lining is that you're getting a substantial slice of the depreciation of the partnership's assets passed back to you each year as well, making these potentially attractive for taxable accounts, if you don't mind the paperwork.

Recent developments on the congressional front may make it possible for mutual funds to own these types of assets and handle the homework and paperwork for you. Should this come about, as now appears likely, this will make holding a diversified and well-researched group of these investments far more convenient for ordinary retail investors.

Individual Corporate or Municipal Bonds

These take on the business risk of owning single enterprises—a hazardous situation if you guess wrong. We recommend that you always err on the side of diversification, both among and within asset classes.

The other risk is that you'll get soaked with high transaction costs when you buy and sell, since an unknown commission is wrapped into the price. Especially with old, small, less-than-top-rated, or infrequently traded issues, the markups can be substantial, and they won't be in your favor.

These caveats don't apply to Treasury bills and bonds, which can be bought directly from our friendly government at **www. treasurydirect.gov** without commission, and which incur no credit risk.

This isn't to say that there aren't any benefits to owning individual bonds. The chief advantage is the ability to count on a precise stream of income and the return of principal when the bond matures (or when it's called)—at least, if the company or municipality hasn't defaulted in the interim. A bond fund's yield will vary, as old bonds are constantly replaced with new ones, and the net asset value when you sell will differ from the net asset value the day you made your purchase, due to intervening interest-rate changes and other factors. Of course, should you have to sell your individual bond prior to maturity for any reason, you'll face the same changes in price due to credit and interest-rate changes. But perhaps you're one of those investors whose plans never change.

As we mentioned earlier, the investment company BlackRock has come closest to solving this problem by offering several closed-end funds that expire at given dates, with the principal returned to shareholders. We hope that someday many more of these will be offered, especially with investment-grade corporate and municipal bonds, so that investors can target their desired maturity and take advantage of economies of scale and diversification in making their purchases, We'd also like you to have the option of buying the bond fund without the addition of leverage.

Smaller investors will have difficulty assembling a diversified portfolio of corporate or municipal bonds for less than $100,000. Here, the bond fund becomes the only answer. However, even large investors may wish to consider parking their fixed-income dollars in no-load, low-expense bond funds.

NOW THAT WE'VE LOOKED at a wide variety of investments, the final chapter will put them together in an income portfolio.

CHAPTER TWELVE

Your Income Portfolio

Growth vs. Income

W e began this book by describing income investing as an alternative to growth or total return investing, especially in an era where the long-term, forward-looking prospects from growth investing appear to be guarded. But it doesn't have to be an either/or situation. As should be clear by now, your authors love diversification, so we recommend doing both: investing for income *and* for growth.

Even the most dedicated income hound will probably want to maintain some exposure (say, 10 or 20 percent of total investable assets, ranging to as high as 50 percent) on the growth side. While the *expected* returns from growth investing are below their historical averages, no one is sure today what the *actual* returns will be. For all anyone knows now, the stock market may be on a rocket ship poised to take off for the stars. We don't think this is likely, but neither do we want to be completely left behind if we're wrong. The vanilla growth portfolio we showed in Figure 2.1 (see page 7) is a fine place to start, and we'll have much more to say about this style of investing in our forthcoming book, *Yes, You Can Still Retire in Comfort!*

After you've decided how much you want to set apart for investing for growth, here are the investment portfolios that we recommend for your income strategy. They should allow you to convert a sum of money into a reliable payout stream: one that is diversified, keeps pace with inflation over the long run, and gives you an optimal yield for the amount of risk you have to assume to get it.

Asset Allocation with Income Investments

Up to this point, we've explored a number of income securities, highlighting some we liked and dismissing others. But how much should you buy of each? This is the thorny question of *asset allocation*, and the answer depends on several factors:

- How active you want to be in managing your investments

- How much yield you require

- How conservative or aggressive you're willing to be in seeking this income (how much risk you're willing to take)

- How concerned you are about inflation eroding your assets over time

The Answer

To meet your income needs, you'll want to broadly diversify into four areas:

1. Real estate investment trusts
2. High-dividend stocks
3. Inflation-protected securities
4. Bonds

These are the four legs of the reclining Barcalounger chair that should provide you with a comfortable lifetime of income.

To decide how much to put into each asset class, we consulted the deepest thinkers in the field of finance, ran the numbers through a means-variance optimizer, and crunched the data through millions of Monte Carlo simulations. We climbed a ziggurat to study the stars, noting their various conjunctions, regressions, and alignments, and then traveled to Tibet and sat at the feet of wise men on snowy Himalayan peaks. Finally, we fed all our findings into a Cray supercomputer and came up with the ultimate answer, shown in Figure 12.1.

Figure 12.1: A Pretty Good Income Allocation

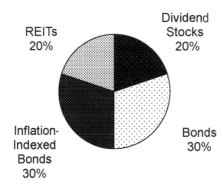

Here's how it stacks up:

- Forty percent of your money goes in stocks and 60 percent in bonds.

- Within the stocks, half should be in real estate investment trusts, and half in high-dividend payers.

- Within the bonds, half should be in inflation-indexed securities, and half in bonds of other kinds.

This allocation is the basic template for all the portfolios that follow.

Which specific investments do you choose to implement it? This will vary according to the level of risk you want to assume. The more income you want, the more risk you have to take. But that said, some trade-offs make more sense than others.

The Conservative Income Portfolio

Imagine that you want to take a leisurely cruise around the world and never once look at the financial pages of a newspaper. Or imagine that you want to treat your income portfolio like a "set-it-and-forget-it" kitchen gadget on a Ronco infomercial. The best choice would be an easy-to-set-up, low expense, passive income portfolio.

The word *passive* has a bad connotation in our action-oriented, youth-worshiping, gotta-have-a-gimmick world, but not in financial economics. "Passive" investments like an S&P 500 Index fund regularly trounce the best active management money can buy. This is due in part to the low expenses and infrequent trading that goes with tracking broad-market indexes, and in part to the efficiency of the market in discounting information into price.

As conservative income investors, you should put 20 percent of your assets into a real estate investment trust index fund, such as one of those found in Table 9.1 (see page 134), and preferably one with a low expense ratio such as Vanguard's REIT Index Fund (ticker: VGSIX) or streetTRACKS Wilshire REIT Index (ticker: RWR) or Cohen & Steers Realty Majors (ticker: ICF).

Put the next 20 percent into the iShares Dow Jones Select Dividend Index Fund (ticker: DVY).

That takes care of your equity allocation.

For bonds, place 30 percent of your assets into a low-expense, inflation-protected securities fund such as those listed in Table 5.4 (see page 43); either Vanguard's (ticker: VISPX) or iShare's (ticker: TIP) are inexpensive choices. As corporate inflation-indexed bond funds come online, you can use these as well.

Finally, place the remaining 30 percent of your money into a high-quality, low-expense, short-term bond mutual fund similar to one of those listed in Table 5.3 (see page 43). An excellent choice would be Vanguard's Short-Term Bond Index Fund (ticker: VBISX), which tracks the Lehman Brothers short-term bond index. This is desirable because, as you've seen, over the long run there's been little benefit attached to going lower in credit quality or longer in maturity than a fund like this delivers.

If this were for a taxable account, a good alternative might be one of the short-term municipal-bond funds from Table 5.11 (see page 64), such as Vanguard's Limited-Term Municipal Bond Fund (ticker: VMLTX). Do-it-yourself folks might want to open an account at **www.treasurydirect.gov** and substitute a five-year ladder or Treasury notes here.

Table 12.1 shows the hypothetical portfolio constructed along these lines.

Table 12.1: A Conservative Income Portfolio 09/2004				
Percent	**Asset**	**Ticker**	**Yield**	**Expense**
REITs				
20%	*Vanguard REIT Index*	VGSIX	4.8%	0.24%
STOCKS				
20%	*iShares Dow Jones Select Dividend*	DVY	3.3%	0.40%
TIPS				
30%	*Vanguard Inflation Protected Securities*	VIPSX	3.5%	0.18%
BONDS				
30%	*Vanguard Short-Term Bond Index*	VBISX	2.9%	0.20%

In setting this up, you'd want to direct Vanguard to distribute your dividends and capital gains to you, rather than reinvesting them back into the funds. Table 12.2 shows an alternate version of this same portfolio constructed entirely with exchange-traded funds, where the dividends would be distributed to you by default:

Table 12.2: A Conservative ETF Income Portfolio 09/2004				
Percent	Asset	Ticker	Current Yield	Expense
REITs				
20%	*Wilshire REIT Index*	RWR	5.1%	0.26%
STOCKS				
20%	*iShares Dow Jones Select Dividend*	DVY	3.3%	0.40%
TIPS				
30%	*iShares Treasury Inflation Protected Sec.*	TIP	4.9%	0.20%
BONDS				
30%	*iShares Lehman 1–3 Year Treasury Bonds*	SHY	1.9%	0.15%

Since the TIP and DVY funds are relatively new, we don't have trailing 12-month yields for them, so the yields shown in Tables 12.1 and 12.2 aren't directly comparable. Do not assume that iShares' TIP will have a higher yield than Vanguard's VIPSX.

Taking the first as illustrative, it generated a 3.8 percent annual yield. It can cost less than $10 to establish and has a super low total annual expense ratio of 0.24 percent. Another way of looking at the expenses is that this portfolio costs you roughly $1 in fees of various kinds to put each $16 of income into your pockets.

In terms of risk, the portfolio value will fluctuate from month to month, but far less than a similarly weighted growth portfolio comprising the S&P 500 and the Lehman Brothers Aggregate Bond Index—in fact, we estimate that it should fluctuate only about half as much. If inflation takes off, this portfolio should fare better, but it will still be hurt to some degree.

Just for fun, we fed the conservative income portfolio through a "Monte Carlo simulator" (a method for stress-testing a portfolio) and let it go for 25,000 one-year runs. On average, the portfolio grew just under 11.6 percent before inflation but after expenses, assuming that you didn't spend any of the dividends, but just left them in the pot to grow. It had a standard deviation of 5.5 percent, which means that most of the time the portfolio grew somewhere between 6 and 17 percent per year (again, before inflation).

The worst one percent of all cases had the portfolio down one percent for the year. But remember, you're spending the dividends, so the worst one percent of cases would actually have you behind the eight ball by one percent minus whatever the portfolio's yield was that year. In the worst year out of 25,000, the portfolio fell 8.7 percent in value (and would have fallen still more if you took out dividends and subtracted for inflation).

The real message from the Monte Carlo stress test is that this is a pretty conservative portfolio. The years when it loses money are infrequent, and it should grow over time, even after you pull out your dividends for current consumption. It should supply you with an ongoing stream of income that increases as years go by, surpassing inflation. There's a lot to love here.

But even a conservative portfolio isn't carefree. During the crisis of April 2004, this portfolio declined 5.4 percent in a single month. That's the difference between Monte Carlo simulation and Wall Street reality (although it's up 5.8 percent since). By way of comparison, if all your money had been in short-term Treasuries (a super-conservative portfolio, but one with a commensurately small yield), you'd only have been down a little over one percent during that month.

By the time you read this, the yields offered by these specific recommended investments undoubtedly will be different. But the features and benefits, as well as the limitations, of the underlying conservative portfolio should endure.

The yield it presently offers is useful as a snapshot comparison to the yields in the portfolios that follow.

The Moderate Income Portfolio

Are you willing to be more active in monitoring your investments? You should be able to reach a higher yield by taking the time and trouble to hire yourself as your own portfolio manager. You're going to maintain the same asset allocation as before, but move into what we hope will be higher-yielding investments within each category. Here's how:

1. First, instead of putting 20 percent of your money in a REIT index fund, you're going to buy shares in the individual REITs listed in Table 9.3 (see page 159). Or, if you have less money, buy the REITs on the short-list portfolio in Table 9.4 (see page 161).

2. Rather than putting 20 percent into the iShare Dow Jones Dividend Fund, you'll purchase some of the individual dividend stocks listed in Table 7.8 (see page 109). Or, if you don't have that much capital available to invest, use the short-list portfolio in Table 7.9 (see page 109).

3. Keep the 30 percent investment in Treasury Inflation-Indexed Securities, as before. A fund of corporate inflation-indexed securities would work as well, as these come on line.

4. Finally, with the 30 percent allocated to other bonds, you're going to move out on the maturity curve to intermediate-term bonds. While a mutual fund that targets the Lehman Brothers' Aggregate Index is an easy choice, do-it-yourself types might want to purchase their own ten-year bond ladder at **www.treasurydirect.gov**.

Table 12.3 illustrates how to spread out your money among these investments.

Table 12.3: Moderate Income Portfolio 09/2004

Percent	Asset	Ticker	Yield	Expense
REITS				
1%	*United Mobile Homes*	UMH	6.5%	0
1%	*Public Storage*	PSA	3.6%	0
1%	*Kimco Realty*	KIM	4.4%	0
1%	*Regency Realty*	REG	4.5%	0
1%	*New Plan Excel*	NXL	6.6%	0
1%	*Realty Income*	O	5.4%	0
1%	*Commercial Net Lease Realty*	NNN	7.1%	0
1%	*Health Care REIT*	HCN	6.7%	0
1%	*Unversal Health Realty*	UHT	6.6%	0
1%	*Healthcare Realty Trust*	HR	6.5%	0
1%	*Archstone-Smith Trust*	ASN	5.4%	0
1%	*BRE Properties*	BRE	5.1%	0
1%	*Hospitality Properties Trust*	HPT	6.8%	0
1%	*Brandywine Realty Trust*	BDN	6.2%	0
1%	*Duke Realty*	DRE	5.6%	0
1%	*Liberty Property Trust*	LRY	6.1%	0
1%	*Mack-Cali Realty*	CLI	5.7%	0
1%	*Pennsylvania REIT*	PEI	5.6%	0
1%	*Cousins Properties*	CUZ	4.3%	0
1%	*Lexington Properties Trust*	LXP	6.4%	0

Table 12.3: Moderate Income Portfolio 09/2004 (cont'd.)

Percent	Asset	Ticker	Yield	Expense
STOCKS				
10%	*iShares DJ Select Dividend Index*	DVY	3.3%	0.40%
1%	*Ameren*	AEE	5.5%	0
1%	*Southern*	SO	4.7%	0
1%	*Peoples Energy*	PGL	5.2%	0
1%	*National Fuel Gas*	NFG	3.9%	0
1%	*SBC Communications*	SBC	4.7%	0
1%	*TrustCo*	TRST	4.7%	0
1%	*Washington Mutual*	WM	4.4%	0
1%	*Unitrin*	UTR	4.0%	0
1%	*ConAgra*	CAG	4.1%	0
1%	*Deluxe*	DLX	3.6%	0
TIPS				
30%	*Vanguard Inflation Protected Sec.*	VIPSX	3.5%	0.18%
BONDS				
30%	*Vanguard Total Bond Market Index*	VBMFX	4.4%	0.22%

For taking the trouble to buy individual stocks and REITs, plus extending your maturity in the bond market, your yield increases from 3.8 percent to 4.3 percent at present. The setup cost to buy the stocks is a one-time expense, possibly less than $400, while the annual expense ratio drops in half to 0.12 percent. This means you're getting nearly $36 in income for every $1 you spend on expenses—an even better ratio than that of the conservative portfolio.

You earn this higher yield in part by concentrating your equity holdings in some specific stocks that we think will be more productive for income-oriented investors. While their historical achievement could regress to the mean, we believe that the performance of the group should more than make up for any bad apples in the barrel.

Table 12.4 shows an abbreviated, minimalist version of the moderate portfolio. Its yield is slightly higher (4.4 percent) than its twin portfolio, no doubt because it's slightly less diversified.

It has the same annual expense ratio, although it requires fewer commissions to set it up initially.

Table 12.4: Minimal Moderate Income Portfolio 09/2004				
Percent	**Asset**	**Ticker**	**Yield**	**Expense**
REITS				
2.5%	*United Mobile Homes*	UMH	6.5%	0
2.5%	*Kimco Realty*	KIM	4.4%	0
2.5%	*Realty Income*	O	5.4%	0
2.5%	*Healthcare Realty Trust*	HR	6.5%	0
2.5%	*Archstone-Smith Trust*	ASN	5.4%	0
2.5%	*Mack-Cali Realty*	CLI	5.7%	0
2.5%	*Hospitality Properties Trust*	HPT	6.8%	0
2.5%	*Cousins Properties*	CUZ	4.3%	0
STOCKS				
10%	*iShares DJ Select Dividend Index*	DVY	3.3%	0.40%
2%	*Ameren*	AEE	5.5%	0
2%	*National Fuel Gas*	NFG	3.9%	0
2%	*SBC Communications*	SBC	5.3%	0
2%	*TrustCo Bank*	TRST	4.7%	0
2%	*Unitrin*	UTR	4.0%	0
TIPS				
30%	*Vanguard Inflation Protected Sec.*	VIPSX	3.5%	0.18%
BONDS				
30%	*Vanguard Total Bond Market Index*	VBMFX	4.4%	0.22%

The risks of these portfolios are less than those lurking in a growth portfolio of a similarly weighted S&P 500 Index and Lehman Brothers Aggregate Bond Index. Their defensive characteristics are similar to the conservative portfolio above, with the exception that they take on more individual-company risk and extend the bond maturities. On the other hand, the individual companies have been selected for their recession resistance and inflation-beating historical performance, so whether these portfolios would actually prove riskier going forward remains to be seen. For a worst-case scenario, in April 2004, the moderate portfolio was down 5.4 percent—the same as the conservative portfolio.

The Aggressive Income Portfolio

The aggressive income portfolio is like the conservative portfolio on steroids, only in this case the muscle booster is leverage.

For the REIT index fund, you substitute a leveraged REIT fund, putting 20 percent of your nest egg in one of the leveraged REIT income funds from Table 9.5 (see page 162).

For dividend income, you employ one of the leveraged dividend funds from Table 8.3 (see page 126). This has the advantage of being able to be held in a taxable account and qualify for the top-dividend tax rate of 15 percent. Alternatively, if the unleveraged Alpine Dynamic Dividend Fund (ticker: ADVDX) proves to deliver a high yield after taxes and expenses, this would be another strong contender.

The only way to increase the inflation-protected-securities performance is to hold fewer of them. The TIPS yield is always going to be low because of the expense of the built-in inflation-insurance policy. We hate for you to set down this shield, so let's keep the TIPS anchored at 30 percent of the portfolio and look to make your extra money elsewhere. When corporate inflation-indexed bond funds arrive, these would be appropriate as well, and should have a slightly higher yield than the Treasury issues.

As for the rest of the bonds, dip a corner of your bread into the emerging markets for some gravy, while putting the remainder into investment-grade corporate bonds. Pimco's leveraged Corporate Income Fund (ticker: PCN) has a 10 percent exposure to emerging-market bonds and an overall credit rating of BBB (investment grade), making it (or its sister fund, Pimco Corporate Opportunity Fund, ticker: PTY) an excellent aggressive choice. Readers who pay high taxes might wish to substitute a leveraged national municipal bond fund here, such as one of those found in Table 6.5 (see page 84). We substituted a taxable corporate bond fund in our example here to facilitate comparison with the more conservative and moderate portfolios above.

Table 12.5 shows the components of this aggressive income portfolio.

Table 12.5: Aggressive Income Portfolio 09/2004				
Percent	**Asset**	**Ticker**	**Current Yield**	**Expense**
REITs				
20%	Cohen & Steers Quality Income	RQI	7.7%	1.1%
STOCKS				
20%	John Hancock Patriot Premium Div.	PDF	6.9%	1.9%
TIPS				
30%	iShares TIPs	TIP	4.9%	0.2%
BONDS				
30%	Pimco Corporate Income Fund	PCN	8.5%	1.2%

At a time when your passbook savings account gets you a nominal return of 0.7 percent, this aggressive portfolio gets you a current yield of 6.9 percent. Setup costs are slight, although your annual expense ratio is higher: 1 percent—or $1 spent for every $7 in income. With 70 percent of your assets subject to leverage (the TIPS fund being the sole exception), this is a large bet on a positively sloped yield curve.

If the yield curve flattens or inverts, or if your borrowing costs exceed your returns from the underlying securities, you'd better be prepared for some rough weather in terms of the net asset value of your leveraged investments. For example, during the monsoon of April 2004, this portfolio was down 11.1 percent, although it rallied very smartly in the summer of 2004 as it became clear that interest rates weren't going in any direction especially fast. Meanwhile, the dividends continued to be paid throughout. That April loss would presumably be an irrelevant figure as to what you'd receive in payments as you went to the mailbox every month.

Table 12.6 compares these three portfolios along three vital dimensions—their yields, their expenses, and how they fared during that cruelest month—to give a real-world sense of what you might expect. Note how they recovered rapidly after April. The moderate portfolio seems to have the best combination of features, but the one that suits you best will depend on your personal needs.

Table 12.6: Income Portfolio Comparison 09/2004				
Portfolio	**Yield**	**April 2004**	**May–Sept 2004**	**Expense**
Conservative	3.8%	-5.4%	+5.8%	0.24%
Moderate	4.3%	-5.9%	+5.1%	0.12%
Aggressive	6.9%*	-11.6%	+8.4%	1.00%

Current Yield, not Trailing 12-Month Yield

Intermediate Positions

These three portfolios—conservative, moderate, and aggressive—can be blended to suit your taste. You can mix and match and cut and paste to your heart's content. They should be good starting points, and here are some of the directions you could take them:

- Hold all the REITs in the intermediate portfolio and put some of your assets into the leveraged REIT fund for added kicks. Alternately, you could buy one of the REIT index funds for diversification—you could even do both. No one from the SEC will come to arrest you.

- Buy the individual dividend stocks as part of your equity portfolio, but also add one of the leveraged preferred funds.

- Keep a fixed portfolio anchored in short-term, high-quality bonds, but also hold a dash of emerging-market bonds and single-state leveraged municipal bonds for the added dose of income.

- Purchase one of the foreign-bond funds from Table 6.1 (see page 73) to diversify away from the U.S. dollar, which many experts believe is poised to fall further.

The point isn't that we've outlined the most brilliant income portfolios in the world, or the most magnificent specific investments to employ. The idea is to be aware of the income options available to you, understand the risk-reward trade-offs they contain, stay highly diversified, and create a portfolio that provides you with income while also letting you sleep at night, erring on the side of caution.

Taxes

Tax-sheltered accounts such as Keoghs, 401(k)s, IRAs, and the like should be stocked first with Treasury Inflation-Protected Securities. This surrenders their exemption from state taxes but also avoids the possible nightmare of having to pay taxes on income you never received.

The next choice for tax-sheltered accounts should be real estate investment trusts. These throw off a lot of income, much of which is taxable at your top marginal rate.

Any remaining room in your tax-deferred accounts should be used to store taxable bonds. If you run out of space for these, you can make up the difference buying municipal bonds in your taxable accounts. Their yields are advantageous to investors in all but the lowest tax brackets (we'll put a link to a municipal versus taxable bond yield calculator on **www.stein-demuth.com** to help you decide).

Your pure dividend-paying stocks (being taxed at a top rate of 15 percent) can be kept in a taxable account without undue damage. Remember that dividends earned at the 15 percent rate will be taxed as ordinary income at your (higher) marginal rate when pulled out of a tax-qualified account. But even dividends pulled from a taxable account will be taxed at 28 percent if you fall victim to the dread Alternative Minimum Tax (AMT). This is still better than the 35 percent or 39 percent they were taxed at previously.

The AMT was designed as a net to catch high-income taxpayers who were using tax shelters in their tax-avoidance schemes, but now increasing numbers of respectable middle-class taxpayers have entered its grasp due to bracket creep—much to the delight of politicians, who can thus raise taxes without lifting a finger. If you've joined the AMT club, you'll be especially interested in seeking out municipal bonds that are "non-AMT" rated. These have slightly lower yields than AMT-taxed municipal bonds (and so should be avoided by those of you not in this predicament), but give a much better break after taxes. A fund full of AMT-taxable municipal bonds that yields 5 percent tax-free might only yield 3.6 percent after the AMT takes its bite.

Table 12.7 lists a few municipal bond funds that are completely free from securities susceptible to the AMT. These should be on your short list to consider if you've fallen into this particular Venus flytrap. Here's a quick way to screen: If the fund is called a *municipal bond fund*, it can contain any amount of what are called *private-activity municipal bonds* that are taxable in the parallel AMT universe. If the fund is titled a *tax-exempt bond fund*, at least 80 percent of the bonds it holds must be of the non-AMT variety.

Table 12.7: Non-AMT Municipal Bond Funds					
Name	Ticker	Yield	Maturity	Credit	Expense
SHORT TERM					
USAA Tax-Exempt Short-Term	USSTX	2.5%	1.9 yrs	A	0.56%
INTERMEDIATE-TERM					
Scudder Tax-Exempt Intermediate-Term	SCMTX	3.8%	6.4 yrs	AAA	0.69%
USAA Tax-Exempt Intermediate-Term	USATX	4.4%	8.3 yrs	AA	0.51%

Annuities

Retirees seeking income beyond the yields available from these portfolios will want to convert a portion of their holdings into immediate fixed and/or variable annuities. The proportion of your assets to annuitize will depend on a number of factors that will vary from case to case, and should be decided in consultation with your financial advisor and accountant. Some of the relevant issues will be:

- Your present income requirements
- Concern about outliving your assets
- The impact of annnuitizing your assets upon your estate
- The tax status of your various investments
- The rates currently available on fixed annuities
- The expense ratios and hurdle rates of variable annuities

Research by Ibbotson Associates suggests that the optimal division of annuitized assets between fixed and variable lifetime-payout annuities should broadly match the division of unannuitized assets otherwise invested in your growth portfolio. For example, if you've decided upon a classic 60 percent stock/40 percent bond portfolio on the growth side as you begin retirement, you'll want to maintain the same balance of 60 percent variable annuity/40 percent fixed annuity going forward in your annuitized accounts (and not the 40 percent stock/60 percent bond allocation we use in the income portfolios here).

With the addition of annuities, you would have three sources of income from your investments:

1. Dividends and coupons from the income portfolio as described above and throughout this book

2. Capital gains from your growth portfolio, broken off and sold in pieces at regular intervals, for present consumption (more on this in your authors' forthcoming book *Yes, You Can Still Retire in Comfort!*)

3. Regular payouts from your fixed and variable lifetime annuities

Where to Hold the Accounts

It's possible to implement these income portfolios using nothing but closed-end funds, individual stocks, and exchange-traded funds. You can do this under one roof by opening a brokerage account at an existing mutual fund family such as Vanguard or Fidelity, or by opening an account at an online discount broker.

As usual, there are trade-offs. For example, Vanguard's online brokerage services are clunky and they have relatively expensive commissions as online discount brokers go. Against this must be balanced Vanguard's very desirable mutual funds and money market funds and the ease of integration—that is, everything arriving on one monthly statement. For the computer-literate, there's also the possibility of electronically downloading all your transactions into Intuit's *Quicken* or Microsoft's *Money* software. This makes keeping track of your finances and year-end tax preparation a snap.

On the other hand, if you go through an online discount broker, you'll have to pay a commission to buy the open-end mutual funds that you could get directly from the sponsoring mutual-fund companies (such as Vanguard) for free. For maximum savings, you could open accounts at both places (a discount broker and a mutual fund company) and do whatever is cheapest at the time, but this means extra paperwork.

Barron's publishes an excellent review of online brokers every March. Some of the ones they recommended in 2004—further screened here for expenses, hospitality to long-term buy-and-hold investors, overall ease of use by computer nonexperts, and *Quicken*-friendliness—are (in order of preference): Scottrade, HarrisDirect, E*Trade, Fidelity, Ameritrade, and Vanguard.

Rebalancing Your Income Accounts

The boilerplate advice from finance writers is to rebalance your accounts every year: Sell whatever has gone up the most in the last 12 months and use the proceeds to top off whatever has slipped. We don't share the widespread enthusiasm for this ritual, with its attendant commissions, tax consequences, and bookkeeping headaches. The problem with rebalancing is that short-term price movements contain a great deal of market noise, and rebalancing just folds this into your portfolios.

If dividend stocks are up this year, it may be that it's because they're truly worth more, or it may only represent high spirits on the part of irrational investors. If the former, then you'd definitely want to keep them; if the latter, then perhaps you should sell. The problem, however, is telling which from which. If you can discern which market movements are meaningful and which are spurious, then you don't need our book, because undoubtedly you're already one of the richest people in the world.

The pipe dream of rebalancers is that they're forever selling the foamy froth while buying the deep value. However, if efficient market theory is to be believed, there's an equal chance that they're actually selling the value and buying the froth, and an even greater chance that they're doing nothing but spinning their wheels—selling froth to buy still more froth, or unloading value to pick up more value.

Our problem isn't with buying low and selling high—quite the contrary, that's our favorite pastime. But one year is too short a time period to sort out the sheep from the goats. Now, five years? That might make a difference.

The allocations we recommend here can stray fairly far from their targets without dramatically affecting your portfolio's risks and returns. To the extent that the stock side grows at the expense of the bonds, returns and risks should increase proportionately, and to the extent that the bond side waxes while stocks wane, the risks should decrease along with the returns.

We might be inclined to recommend that you rebalance if the portfolio got wildly out of alignment from its targeted allocation (for example, if any of the asset classes wandered 15 percentage points from their moorings). At that point, you'd retune the portfolio back to original factory specifications. It would be surprising, though, if this were necessary more than once every few years, on average.

If you go the route of buying individual stocks (such as in the moderate portfolio), the question arises as to under what circumstances should you sell one of them. You should sell when you have a better investment to take its place. Remember that buying and selling stocks costs money and can have consequences come April 15th, and all of these factors need to be weighed in your decision. But if the yield falls, or the company gets itself into a jam, by all means find a better stock (preferably within the same category) to take its place.

WE HOPE THAT YOU NOW have some better ideas about how to invest for income than you did when you started. We've covered a lot of ground in this book and presented a colossal amount of data. Our intention was not that you should understand and remember everything at once, but that the volume could be placed on your shelf as an ongoing reference tool (used in conjunction with our Website, **www.stein-demuth.com**). There are a lot of financial products out there vying for your investment dollars, and many of them are confusing and expensive. Keep your strategy simple, stick to investments that you understand, and you should do well.

Our next book *(Yes, You Can Still Retire in Comfort!)* will talk in more detail about investing for and during retirement. It will be out from New Beginnings Press in fall 2005, and if you've found this book useful, we hope you'll give it a look as well.

Addendum

Memo to the Mutual Fund Industry: Ten Mutual Funds We'd Like to See

There were 8,126 different mutual funds available to U.S. investors in 2003. Aren't we being a bit piggish to ask for ten more?

Not at all. As we've noted throughout this book, income investors (such as retirees, whose number will soon be legion) have need of very specific income-producing investments to use as building blocks in their portfolios. We've assembled our suggestions below in the hopes that some higher-ups in the mutual fund industry will wake up and smell the money.

In no particular order:

1. **A corporate inflation-linked bond fund:** Instead of mushing the corporate inflation-linked bonds and notes with the current TIPS funds, keep them separate. Putting these corporate bonds into a mutual fund would diversify away the individual business risk, an irrelevant consideration as far as Treasury bonds are concerned. Unlike with the Treasuries, this would be suitable for taxable accounts, because these notes don't generate phantom income. The

fund would have a high yield to compensate for its not being backed by the full faith and credit of the U.S. government. It would also be reasonably secure against interest-rate risk, being hedged against inflation and having a shorter maturity (holding notes under ten years) than the funds built on the longer-term Treasury inflation bonds. Finally, the management company could bring its pricing power to bear on the market and get these bonds for mom-and-pop investors at a reasonable price, unlike if retail investors went shopping for them one by one.

2. **An unleveraged, intermediate-term, tax-exempt, investment-grade-bond index ETF,** and while we're on the subject; 3. **an unleveraged, short-term, tax-exempt investment-grade-bond index ETF:** In extremis, we'd settle for any closed-end fund here. There are presently no municipal-bond index ETFs, while the hundreds of existing municipal closed-end funds out there are leveraged, have long maturities, contain municipal junk bonds, or all three—to say nothing of many of these having high expenses.

These new, lower-risk, tax-exempt bond funds would be great for investors to buy for their taxable accounts, where they'd be gobbled up like M&M's. The sponsoring company could buy the underlying muni bonds with minimal transaction expenses and wafer-thin bid/ask spreads. While there are open-end municipal bond funds such as we propose, unless investors buy them directly from the fund companies themselves, it's difficult to get the income distributed, as it's usually reinvested by default (where it adds to the assets under management upon which the sponsor's fees are based). Closed-end bond funds and ETFs distribute their coupons by default, which is how income investors like it.

These could start as national municipal bond funds for maximum diversification, but there's no reason why there couldn't be regional funds for high-tax states as well. There could also be AMT and non-AMT iterations to fit the tax status of the investor. But for now, any tax-exempt bond ETF would be welcome.

4. **The diversified risky-asset income fund:** Here, at least, the mutual-fund companies have an excuse—some of these assets can't at present be legally held in a mutual fund (which may be about to change). This simply points out the need for the Daddy Warbucks types who run the mutual fund industry to lobby Congress to get the laws changed the way income investors want them!

    The diversified risky-asset income fund would buy the very investments we told you to avoid earlier: mortgage REITs, business-development companies, master limited partnerships, royalty trusts, even the occasional high-yield bond. This would be a closed-end fund with an astute research team to sift out the scammers, flimflammers, and bamboozlers, and select only those businesses with a sincere desire to pay shareholders a big dividend.

    After this fundamental screening, risk would further be diversified by owning different types of businesses, whose fortunes presumably would be uncorrelated to some degree. Finally, the mutual fund would figure out all the tax angles and K-1s, mailing a simple no muss, no fuss Form 1099 to file at year-end, just as you'd receive from any other mutual fund.

5. **The REIT income fund:** Sure, there are lots of closed-end funds that use REITs for income, but none with the methodology we advocate to pick those most suitable for true income investors: a steady,

long-term, inflation-beating payout, provided in the wrapper of an unleveraged ETF or closed-end fund. Fund managers could keep the portfolio up-to-date by following the principles we advocate, greatly simplifying life for those looking to REITs for a steady paycheck.

6. The same holds true for our **diversified dividend equity fund.** We've seen that iShares' DVY comes close, but why not have a fund that gives investors the best of all possible worlds: the steady payers, the regular raisers, and the highest dividend payers diversified across industry groups? As with the REIT income fund above, a manager who followed the method we espouse could profitably run such a fund every month in less time than it takes to play 18 holes of golf. *Special bonus fund:* A foreign-language version of the same that specialized in dividend stocks from other countries would be snapped up by investors eager to diversify against a falling U.S. dollar.

7. **A laddered corporate-bond fund;** and 8. **a laddered tax-exempt bond fund:** Astonishingly, no one offers a closed-end fund that simply ladders corporate or municipal bonds (where, unlike with Treasury bonds, a mutual fund is needed for pricing power and diversification). These new, low-expense-index, exchange-traded funds offering one-stop shopping for a five- or a ten-year bond ladder would be pounced upon by income investors like raw red meat. (We even propose a name: LADDERS.)

9. **An unleveraged, true preferred stock income fund:** This one is a bit esoteric, but stay with us. Nearly all the preferred funds currently available include hybrid-trust preferreds, which aren't taxed at the low 15 percent dividend tax rate. Our new

fund would solve this problem by banishing all trust preferreds from its stock-selection universe. Additionally, preferred stocks are already highly sensitive to interest rate risk—so let's get rid of the leverage and deal with one risk at a time, please.

A fund is desirable here because of its power to diversify away the individual business risk of owning preferreds singly. Presumably management could bring some research skills to bear on the selection process and even buy some of the many preferreds that aren't traded on major exchanges and are found only in places where individual investors fear to tread.

10. Where, oh where, is the unhedged basket of **foreign-currencies fund?** We aren't alone in thinking that the U.S. dollar may be destined to fall in coming years against other currencies. All we're asking for is an unleveraged, low-expense, exchange-traded index fund that tracks a composite mix of euros, yen, and the like. Short-term international bonds would be fine. The dividend might be small, but the diversification of currency risk (and, ultimately, purchasing-power risk) would make this a worthwhile trade-off for income investors.

Mutual fund management companies, we look forward to hearing from you.

About the Authors

Ben Stein can be seen talking about finance on Fox TV news every week and writing about it regularly in *The New York Times* Sunday business section. No wonder: Not only is he the son of the world-famous economist and government adviser Herbert Stein, but Ben is a respected economist in his own right. He received his B.A. with honors in economics from Columbia University in 1966, studied the subject in the graduate school of economics at Yale while he earned his law degree there as valedictorian of the class of 1970, and worked as an economist for the Department of Commerce.

Ben is known to many as a movie and television personality, especially from *Ferris Bueller's Day Off* and his long-running quiz show, *Win Ben Stein's Money*, but he's probably worked more in personal and corporate finance than anything else. He's written about finance for *Barron's* and *The Wall Street Journal* for decades. He was one of the chief busters of the junk-bond frauds of the 1980s, has been a longtime critic of corporate executives' self-dealing, and has written three self-help books about personal finance. He frequently travels the country speaking about finance in both serious and humorous ways, and has been a regular contributor to the AARP's *Modern Maturity* (now *AARP: The Magazine*). He is co-author with Phil DeMuth of *Yes, You Can Time the Market!*

Website: **www.benstein.com**

⊞⊞⊞

Phil DeMuth was the valedictorian of his class at the University of California at Santa Barbara in 1972, then took his master's in communications and Ph.D. in clinical psychology. Both a psychologist and registered investment advisor, Phil has written for *The Wall Street Journal, Barron's,* and **forbes.com,** as well as *Human Behavior* and *Psychology Today.* His opinions have been quoted in **theStreet.com,** *On Wall Street,* and *Fortune* magazine. He is president of Conservative Wealth Management in Los Angeles, a registered investment counsel to high-net-worth individuals and their families.

Website: **www.phildemuth.com**

■ Investment Notes ■

■ Investment Notes ■

✚ Investment Notes ✚

⊞ Investment Notes ⊞

■ Investment Notes ■

✚ Investment Notes ✚

NBP

We hope you enjoyed this book.
If you'd like additional information, please contact
New Beginnings Press through their distributors:

Hay House, Inc.
P.O. Box 5100
Carlsbad, CA 92018-5100

(760) 431-7695 or **(800) 654-5126**
(760) 431-6948 (fax) or **(800) 650-5115 (fax)**
www.hayhouse.com®

Published and distributed in Australia by: Hay House Australia
Pty. Ltd. • 18/36 Ralph St. • Alexandria NSW 2015 • *Phone:* 612-
9669-4299 • *Fax:* 612-9669-4144 • www.hayhouse.com.au

Published and distributed in the United Kingdom by:
Hay House UK, Ltd. • Unit 62, Canalot Studios •
222 Kensal Rd., London W10 5BN • *Phone:* 44-20-8962-
1230 • *Fax:* 44-20-8962-1239 • www.hayhouse.co.uk

*Published and distributed in the Republic of South Africa
by:* Hay House SA (Pty), Ltd., P.O. Box 990, Witkoppen 2068
• *Phone/Fax:* 27-11-706-6612 • orders@psdprom.co.za

Published in India by: Hay House Publications (India) Pvt.
Ltd., 3 Hampton Court, A-Wing, 123 Wodehouse Rd., Colaba,
Mumbai 400005 • *Phone:* 91 (22) 22150557 or 22180533 •
Fax: 91 (22) 22839619 • www.hayhouseindia.com

Distributed in India by: Media Star, 7 Vaswani Mansion,
120 Dinshaw Vachha Rd., Churchgate, Mumbai
400020 • *Phone:* 91 (22) 22815538-39-40 • *Fax:* 91 (22)
22839619 • booksdivision@mediastar.co.in

Distributed in Canada by: Raincoast • 9050
Shaughnessy St., Vancouver, B.C. V6P 6E5 •
Phone: (604) 323-7100 • *Fax:* (604) 323-2600